ADDITIONAL ACCLAIM

"Stephen Porges, PhD, has not only made one of the most profound and illuminating contributions to our understanding of nervous system in the last 50 years—he's made one of the most useful ones. Anyone who works with people, or who seeks to heal others, can benefit from his insights. Porges has helped cracked the facial code, and deepened our understanding as to the relationships between our nervous system, our facial expressions, and bodily sensations. There has been brilliant work on the relationship between facial expressions and the emotions by Darwin and Ekman. Porges extends these discoveries inward, relating them to the nervous system. What is so special about his contribution is that it is of immediate clinical import. His principles and discoveries guide us as to how, and when, to intervene in some of the most challenging clinical conditions, and opens up new kinds of treatment possibilities. For decades he's written as a scientist for scientists. Now, in this clear, accessible book, which is an ideal introduction to his ideas, we see what it is like to be in conversation with this brilliant man. This is ideal for clinicians of any kind, but also for anyone who wants to better understand their own nervous system, and that of those they care about."

—NORMAN DOIDGE, MD, AUTHOR, THE BRAIN THAT CHANGES ITSELF, AND THE BRAIN'S WAY OF HEALING

In The Pocket Guide to the Polyvagal Theory, *Stephen Porges succeeds, as few researchers do, in the art of deconstructing dense scientific concepts to render them wonderfully accessible to clients, clinicians, and the lay person alike. As the subtleties of the Polyvagal Theory are brought to life through the friendly voice of an innovative genius, a new understanding about the influence of the autonomic nervous system on human behavior emerges, along with neurobiological explanations for a variety of difficulties. You will find that many of the perplexing issues that bring clients to therapy suddenly make biological sense, as well as discover the seeds of bottom-up roadmaps for healing them. Read this book, and be inspired by a revolutionary perspective on the human condition that will have a far-reaching positive impact on your life, your relationships, and your clinical practice."*

—PAT OGDEN, PHD, FOUNDER/EDUCATIONAL DIRECTOR, SENSORIMOTOR PSYCHOTHERAPY INSTITUTE, BOULDER, COLORADO USA

THE NORTON SERIES ON INTERPERSONAL NEUROBIOLOGY

Louis Cozolino, PhD, Series Editor
Allan N. Schore, PhD, Series Editor, 2007–2014
Daniel J. Siegel, MD, Founding Editor

The field of mental health is in a tremendously exciting period of growth and conceptual reorganization. Independent findings from a variety of scientific endeavors are converging in an interdisciplinary view of the mind and mental well-being. An interpersonal neurobiology of human development enables us to understand that the structure and function of the mind and brain are shaped by experiences, especially those involving emotional relationships.

The Norton Series on Interpersonal Neurobiology provides cutting-edge, multidisciplinary views that further our understanding of the complex neurobiology of the human mind. By drawing on a wide range of traditionally independent fields of research—such as neurobiology, genetics, memory, attachment, complex systems, anthropology, and evolutionary psychology—these texts offer mental health professionals a review and synthesis of scientific findings often inaccessible to clinicians. The books advance our understanding of human experience by finding the unity of knowledge, or consilience, that emerges with the translation of findings from numerous domains of study into a common language and conceptual framework. The series integrates the best of modern science with the healing art of psychotherapy.

A NORTON PROFESSIONAL BOOK

STEPHEN W. PORGES

THE POCKET GUIDE TO THE POLYVAGAL THEORY

The Transformative Power of Feeling Safe

W. W. NORTON & COMPANY
Independent Publishers Since 1923
New York • London

NOTE TO READERS: Standards of clinical practice and protocol change over time, and no technique or recommendation is guaranteed to be safe or effective in all circumstances. This volume is intended as a general information resource for professionals practicing in the field of psychotherapy and mental health; it is not a substitute for appropriate training, peer review, and/or clinical supervision. Neither the publisher nor the author(s) can guarantee the complete accuracy, efficacy, or appropriateness of any particular recommendation in every respect.

Printed in the United States of America
First Edition

For information about permission to reproduce selections from this book, write to
Permissions, W. W. Norton & Company, Inc.,
500 Fifth Avenue, New York, NY 10110

For information about special discounts for bulk purchases, please contact
W. W. Norton Special Sales at specialsales@wwnorton.com or 800-233-4830

Manufacturing by Lake Book Manufacturing, Inc.
Production manager: Christine Critelli

Library of Congress Cataloging-in-Publication Data

Names: Porges, Stephen W., author.
Title: The pocket guide to the polyvagal theory : the transformative
power of feeling safe / Stephen W. Porges.
Description: New York : W. W Norton & Company, [2017] | Series: A norton
professional book | Includes bibliographical references and index.
Identifiers: LCCN 2017013975 | ISBN 9780393707878 (pbk.)
Subjects: LCSH: Affective neuroscience. | Emotions. | Social interaction. |
Interpersonal relations.
Classification: LCC QP401 .P668 2017 | DDC 612.8/233—dc23
LC record available at https://lccn.loc.gov/2017013975

W. W. Norton & Company, Inc.,
500 Fifth Avenue, New York, N.Y. 10110
www.wwnorton.com

W. W. Norton & Company Ltd.,
15 Carlisle Street, London W1D 3BS

TO THE SURVIVORS OF TRAUMA WHO HEROICALLY SEARCH FOR SAFETY.

CONTENTS

Acknowledgments ix
Preface xiii
Glossary 1

1. The Neurobiology of Feeling Safe 33
2. Polyvagal Theory and the Treatment of Trauma 53
3. Self-Regulation and Social Engagement 97
4. How Polyvagal Theory Explains the Consequences of Trauma on Brain, Body, and Behavior 127
5. Cues of Safety, Health, and Polyvagal Theory 169
6. The Future of Trauma Therapy: A Polyvagal Perspective 199
7. Somatic Perspectives on Psychotherapy 215

References 245
Credits 253

ACKNOWLEDGMENTS

Polyvagal Theory emerged from my research and insights on October 8, 1994 (Porges, 1995). On that date in Atlanta, I described the model with its theoretical implications in my presidential address to the Society for Psychophysiological Research. At that time, I was unaware that the theory would be embraced by clinicians. I had conceptualized the theory as a structure for testable hypotheses within the research community. Consistent with my initial expectations, the theory has had impact in science and has been cited in several thousand peer reviewed publications representing several disciplines. However, the main impact of the theory has been to provide plausible neurophysiological explanations for several of the experiences described by individuals who have experienced trauma. For these individuals the theory provided an understanding of how their bodies were retuned in response to life threat and lost the resilience to return to a state of safety.

Several people have played important roles in helping me translate my ideas into a coherent theory. Foremost, I want to acknowledge my wife, Sue Carter. For more than four decades she has listened, witnessed, and shared ideas that were to become the Polyvagal Theory. Sue's landmark work, discovering the role of oxytocin in social bonds, and her general interest in the neurobiology of social behavior served to focus my thinking on the role the autonomic nervous system and physiological state played in not only health, but also in social behavior. Without Sue's enduring support, love, and intellectual curiosity, Polyvagal Theory would not have evolved. I am sincerely grateful to Sue's contribution.

Unlike many of my colleagues, who treat and study trauma, trauma was not a focus of my research or part of my theoretical agenda. Without traumatologists being interested in Polyvagal Theory, there would not have been an entrée for the theory to contribute to the treatment of trauma. This entrée was due to three pioneers in traumatology, Peter Levine, Bessel van der Kolk, and Pat Ogden. I graciously acknowledge their influence on my work and their generosity in welcoming me on their journey to understand and rehabilitate the disruptive effects of trauma. It was through their passion to help their clients, their commitment to learn, and their curiosity to understand the processes involved in experiencing and recovering from trauma that they embraced insights from the theory into their treatment models.

Through my connections with Peter, Bessel, and Pat, I have participated in dozens of meetings and workshops on trauma. Through these interactions, I became informed about the profound disruptive impact of trauma on a significant portion of the population. I became aware that survivors of trauma often go through life without an opportunity to understand their bodily reaction to the trauma or to recover the ability to regulate and to co-regulate their physiological and behavioral state. Many of these individuals are revictimized when discussing their experiences and often reprimanded for not fighting or fleeing. Others are chastised for not psychologically recovering, when there is no apparent physical damage.

I want to acknowledge the contribution of Theo Kierdorf in the development of this book. The idea for a book based on the transcripts of interviews with clinicians was suggested by Theo. Theo not only was the translator for the German version* of this volume, but also was an active participant in selecting, editing, and organizing most of the material included. I sincerely appreciate his insights and his ability to thematically organize my words and writings. Theo and I worked together on the initial introduction in German of Polyvagal Theory.† Similar to this collaboration, he mentored me in understanding the difference between writing to document and writing to communicate. As a scientist, my focus has been on documentation. Through my interactions with Theo, I have gained a better understanding of how scientific writings can be shaped to enhance communication. I am grateful to Theo for his contributions to this volume and his sincere commitment to making Polyvagal Theory more accessible.

A special thanks to Deborah Malmud, my editor at Norton. Deborah patiently worked with me to transform my manuscript into an accessible vehicle for the Polyvagal Theory.

---

* Porges, S.W. (2017) *Die Polyvagal-Theorie und die Suche nach Sicherheit: Traumabehandlung, soziales Engagement und Bindung.* Lichenau, Germany: G.P. Probst Verlag.

† Porges, S. W. (2010). *Die Polyvagal-Theorie: Neurophysiologische Grundlagen der Therapie.* Paderborn, Germany: Junfermann Verlag.

PREFACE

WHY A BOOK OF CONVERSATIONS?

When *The Polyvagal Theory: Neurophysiological Foundations of Emotions, Attachment, Communication, and Self-Regulation** was published, it provided a vehicle to archive the scientific basis of the theory. The book made accessible to clinicians and other professionals a Polyvagal perspective that provided new concepts and insights for understanding human behavior. The perspective placed an emphasis on the important link between psychological experiences and physical manifestations in the body. The book was dense and written for scientists. As a collection of edited papers that had previously been published in scientific journals and academic books, the book provided easy access to work that would have been buried in specialty literature. Thus, I was pleased to have my work lifted from the obscurity of the scientific publications with their limited and often costly distribution to public portals such as Amazon.

When I wrote the book, my goal was to archive the docu-

* Porges, S. W. (2011). *The polyvagal theory: Neurophysiological foundations of emotions, attachment, communication, and self-regulation.* Norton series on interpersonal neurobiology. New York, NY: W. W. Norton.

ments that formed the corpus of the theory. What followed the publication was not anticipated. To my surprise, the book has sold well and is being read by professionals in many different disciplines. It has been translated into German, Italian, Spanish, and Portuguese. It has helped to kindle interest in Polyvagal Theory, which has resulted in my participation in webinars and invited presentations at conferences in many countries. This interest in Polyvagal Theory has come with a request to make the theory more accessible to clinicians and their clients. I have frequently been told how dense (difficult) the book is to read and in the same interaction been told how accessible I have made these same ideas in my talks. I normally respond by saying that when I give talks, my objective is to communicate, and when I write papers, my objective is to convey data and ideas within the constraints of scientific publications.

During the past few years, at the prompting of many clinicians, it has become clear to me that I have a responsibility to deconstruct the dense content of the theory into a written style that will be more accessible. This book is a product of this urging. I approached the problem of translation by reviewing the transcripts of several of my interviews. Since the interviews were conducted by clinicians, the focus of my responses was on clinical applications.

The interviews follow a glossary familiarizing readers with the constructs and concepts embedded in Polyvagal Theory as well as an introductory chapter providing a discussion of the science and the scientific culture in which Polyvagal Theory was developed. The interviews have been edited to improve completeness and clarity. The interview format provides a spontaneous and informal vehicle to communicate clinically relevant features of Polyvagal Theory. The interviews have been selected to provide clinicians with an understanding of how our nervous system adapts to challenges and to enable therapists to develop therapeutic strategies to rehabilitate biobehavioral regulation through social interactions. The transcripts have been edited to reduce redundancy and to keep the flow of the discussions focused. In places, my responses have been expanded and clarified. The reader will note that rather than reducing all redundancy, several themes are discussed within the contexts of the different interviews. Reintroducing themes central to Polyvagal Theory within these different contexts provided an opportunity to expand meaning and clinical relevance.

WHY FOCUS ON OUR QUEST FOR SAFETY?

My exposure to the clinical world has motivated me to communicate the novel and relevant perspectives of Polyvagal Theory in a more accessible form. My talks have focused on how the regulation of the autonomic nervous system functions as a neural platform upon which different classes of adaptive behavior could be efficiently expressed. Polyvagal Theory emphasizes that evolution provides an organizing principle to identify neural circuits that promoted social behavior and two classes of defensive strategies, mobilization associated with fighting or fleeing and immobilization associated with hiding or feigning death. The phylogenetically most recent mammalian circuit fosters social behavior and is defined by a face–heart connection in which the neural regulation of the striated muscles of our face and head are neurophysiologically linked to the neural regulation of our heart. According to Polyvagal Theory, the face–heart connection provides humans and other mammals with an integrated social engagement system that detects and projects features of "safety" to conspecifics through facial expressions and vocalizations that are covariates of autonomic state. Within this model, how we look, listen, and vocalize conveys information about whether we are safe to approach.

Recently, after I was interviewed on a webinar, listeners posted comments on a blog. When I read their comments, I realized that the listeners understood Polyvagal Theory in a language that transcended the complexity of science. Despite my training as a scientist and the pragmatic way in which I was trained to write scientific papers, the casual conversation of the webinar provided an effective and accessible vehicle to convey the essence of the theory. As the listeners processed the hour-long interview, the message that was distilled was simply that a quest for safety is the basis for living a successful life.

In writing this book, it is my hope to highlight the important role of feeling safe as an important component of the healing process. From a Polyvagal perspective, deficits in feeling safe form the core biobehavioral feature that leads to mental and physical illness. It is my sincere hope that furthering an understanding of our need to feel safe will lead to new social, educational, and clinical strategies that will enable us to become more welcoming as we invite others to co-regulate on a quest for safety.

THE POCKET GUIDE TO THE POLYVAGAL THEORY

GLOSSARY

Adaptive behavior. Polyvagal Theory emphasizes the adaptive function of spontaneous behaviors by focusing on the impact that behavior has on regulating physiological state. This perspective is based on an evolutionary model in which behavior is interpreted as adaptive if it enhances survival, minimizes distress, or influences physiological state in a manner that would optimize health, growth, and restoration. At times behaviors that are initially adaptive may become maladaptive. For example, this would occur if an acute behavior that initially enhanced survival or minimized distress during threat is chronically recruited when there is no threat. Such a behavior would be maladaptive, since it would not optimize survival and may compromise physiological function and amplify distress. Trauma may result in reactions that are initially adaptive in a life threat situation (e.g., immobilizing and passing out), which if repeated or slightly modified (e.g., dissociation) in less threatening situations will be maladaptive.
See pages: 43, 45, 55–56, 61, 67, 73, 99, 122, 139, 141–142, 156, 176–178, 195, 200, 202, 205, 209, 212, 229, 241–242

Afferent nerves. Polyvagal Theory focuses on a subset of afferent fibers that send information from the visceral organs to brain structures. These pathways are also called sensory nerves, because they send signals from organs informing brainstem regulatory structures of the status of the organs.
See: throughout

Anxiety. Anxiety is frequently defined from a psychological (emotional feelings of fear or uneasiness) or psychiatric (e.g., anxiety disorders) perspective. Polyvagal Theory emphasizes the autonomic state that underlies the psychological feelings that define anxiety. Polyvagal Theory assumes that anxiety is dependent on an autonomic state characterized by concurrent activation of the sympathetic nervous system with a down-regulation of the 'ventral' vagal circuit (see ventral vagal complex) and the social engagement system (see social engagement system).
See pages: 97, 153, 160, 191–193, 200, 216

Attachment. Attachment is a psychological construct reflecting a strong emotional bond between two individuals, such as the relationship between a mother and her child. Polyvagal Theory focuses on the features of safety manifested in the social engagement system (see social engagement system) that enable attachment to occur. Prosodic voices, positive facial expressions, and welcoming gestures trigger through neuroception (see neuroception) feelings of safety and trust that spontaneously emerge when the social engagement system is activated.
See pages: 72–73, 99, 122–123, 183, 230

Autism. Autism spectrum disorder (ASD) is a complex psychiatric diagnosis that includes communication problems and

difficulties relating to people. Polyvagal Theory focuses on the observation that a diagnosis of ASD involves features that reflect a depressed social engagement system (see social engagement system). Thus, many individuals with ASD have voices without prosody, have auditory hypersensitivities, have auditory processing difficulties, do not make good eye contact, have flat facial expressivity especially in the upper part of their faces, and have severe behavioral state regulation difficulties that are frequently manifested in tantrums. Polyvagal Theory is not focused on the antecedent cause of these problems, but takes an optimistic perspective and assumes that many of the features of the depressed social engagement system observed in ASD may be reversed through an understanding of how the nervous system, via neuroception, responds to cues of safety. Intervention strategies based on the Polyvagal Theory emphasize re-engagement of the social engagement system. Polyvagal Theory does not make any assumptions regarding features in ASD other than a depressed social engagement system.
See pages: 74-76, 79-80, 87-88, 97, 116, 119, 127, 136, 206-211, 221

Autonomic balance. Autonomic balance is a construct that represents the balance between the sympathetic and parasympathetic branches of the autonomic nervous system. Although several organs receive innervation from both branches of the autonomic nervous system, autonomic balance assumes a linear additive model in which both branches have similar magnitudes of influence. For example, since the sympathetic nervous system increases heart rate and the parasympathetic nervous system decreases heart rate through the vagus (the major neural component of the parasympathetic nervous system), a high heart rate would be interpreted as a manifestation of an autonomic balance biased towards sympathetic excitation. In contrast, a slow heart rate would be interpreted as a bias towards parasympathetic excitation.

Although autonomic balance is a frequently used term, it is often used to indicate dysfunction in the autonomic nervous system (e.g., atypical autonomic balance). From a Polyvagal perspective, a focus on autonomic balance obfuscates the importance of the phylogenetically-ordered response hierarchy of how the autonomic nervous system reacts to challenges. According to Polyvagal Theory, when the social engagement system with the myelinated ventral vagal pathways is engaged, a unique autonomic state emerges that supports an optimal autonomic balance in the regulation of subdiaphragmatic organs. This optimal autonomic balance to subdiaphragmatic organs, via sympathetic and unmyelinated dorsal vagal pathways, is the emergent product of the activation of the ventral vagal pathways. Due to the hierarchical nature of autonomic reactivity, activation of ventral vagal pathways enables both branches of the autonomic nervous system regulating subdiaphragmatic organs from being engaged in defense.

See pages: 58, 172, 224–225

Autonomic nervous system [traditional view]. The autonomic nervous system is the part of the nervous system that regulates the internal organs in the body without conscious awareness. The name reflects that the regulation occurs in an "automatic" manner. Traditional definitions partition the autonomic nervous system into two subsystems: the sympathetic nervous system and the parasympathetic nervous system. Traditional views emphasize the antagonistic influence of the motor pathways of the sympathetic and parasympathetic nervous systems traveling to the target organs and do

not emphasize the sensory pathways traveling from the organs to the brain or the brainstem areas regulating both sensory and motor pathways that provide the bidirectional communication between the internal organs and the brain.
See pages: 58–59, 171, 223–224

Autonomic nervous system [Polyvagal Theory]. Polyvagal Theory focuses on the vagus, the primary component of the parasympathetic nervous system. The vagus is the tenth cranial nerve, which connects brainstem areas to several visceral organs. The theory emphasizes the difference between two motor (efferent) pathways that travel through the vagus; each pathway originates in a different area of the brainstem (i.e., dorsal nucleus of the vagus and nucleus ambiguus). The primary motor pathways from the dorsal motor nucleus of the vagus (i.e. dorsal vagus) are unmyelinated and terminate in visceral organs located below the diaphragm (i.e., subdiaphragmatic vagus). The primary motor pathways from the nucleus ambiguus (i.e., ventral vagus) are myelinated and terminate in in visceral organs located above the diaphragm (i.e. supradiaphragmatic vagus).

Polyvagal Theory uses a more inclusive definition of the autonomic nervous system that includes sensory pathways and emphasizes the brainstem areas regulating autonomic function. The theory links the brainstem regulation of the ventral vagus to the regulation of the striated muscles of the face and head to produce an integrated social engagement system (see Figure 1, ventral vagal complex and social engagement system).

In contrast to the traditional model that focuses on chronic influences on visceral organs, Polyvagal Theory emphasizes autonomic reactivity. Polyvagal Theory accepts the traditional model of interpreting chronic autonomic influences on visceral organs as the sum of a paired antagonism between vagal and sympathetic pathways. However, Polyvagal Theory proposes a phylogenetically ordered hierarchy in which autonomic subsystems react to challenges in the reverse of their evolutionary history consistent with the principle of dissolution (see dissolution).

The theory postulates that when the ventral vagus and the associated social engagement system are optimally functioning, the autonomic nervous system supports health, growth, and restoration. During this ventral vagal state, there is an optimal 'autonomic balance' between the sympathetic nervous system and the dorsal vagal pathways to subdiaphragmatic organs. When the function of the ventral vagus is dampened or withdrawn the autonomic nervous system is optimized to support defense and not health. According to the Polyvagal Theory, these defense reactions may be manifested as either an increase in sympathetic activity that would inhibit the function of the dorsal vagus to promote mobilization strategies such as fight and flight behaviors or as a biobehavioral shutdown manifested as depressed sympathetic activation and a surge of dorsal vagal influences that would result in fainting, defecation, and an inhibition of motor behavior often seen in mammals feigning death. **See pages:** 40, 48-49, 51, 62-65, 68-69, 99, 101–102, 104, 107, 127-131, 141, 157, 164-165, 171-174, 184, 223-228

Autonomic state. Within Polyvagal Theory autonomic state and physiological state are interchangeable constructs. Polyvagal Theory describes three primary circuits that provide neural regulation of autonomic state; these states are selectively regulated by ventral vagal, dorsal vagal, and sympathetic pathways. Autonomic state reflects activation of these pathways. In

general, there is a focus on each circuit providing the primary neural regulation for a specific state. This would result in the ventral vagal circuit supporting social engagement behaviors, the sympathetic nervous system supporting mobilized defensive (fight/flight) behaviors, and the dorsal vagal circuit supporting immobilized defensive behaviors. However, autonomic state can support mobilization and immobilization behaviors that are not defensive when coupled with activation of the ventral vagal circuit and the social engagement system (see autonomic balance and social engagement system). Thus, by coupling the social engagement system with the sympathetic nervous system there is an opportunity to mobilize without moving into defense. This is observed in play in which aggressive movements are contained by social engagement behaviors. Similarly, when the social engagement system is coupled with the dorsal vagal circuit, cues of safety (e.g., prosodic voice, facial expression) enable immobilization to occur without recruiting defense (e.g., shutdown, behavioral collapse, dissociation). This is observed during intimacy and in trusting relationships. Thus, through the coupling of social engagement with mobilization and immobilization, the three autonomic circuits support five states associated with different classes of behavior: social engagement, fight/flight, play, shutdown, and intimacy.
See pages: 39, 41, 44-45, 50-51, 68, 75, 83, 105, 117, 156, 164, 219

Biological imperative. Biological imperatives are the needs of living organisms required to perpetuate their existence. This list frequently includes survival, territorialism, fitness, and reproduction. Polyvagal Theory emphasizes that the need to connect with others is a primary biological imperative for humans. The theory emphasizes that through connectedness, physiology is

co-regulated to optimize mental and physical health. The theory focuses on the role that the social engagement system plays in initiating and maintaining connectedness and co-regulation.
See pages: 50–51, 182, 195

Biological rudeness. Our nervous system evolved to anticipate reciprocal interactions from others when the social engagement system down regulates autonomic nervous system defenses via the ventral vagus. When this neural expectancy is violated, by either a neglect of the engagement cues or a hostile reaction, there is an immediate and massive shift in the autonomic nervous system to a state that supports defense. This violation frequently promotes an emotional response of being hurt and a personal narrative of being offended. Biological rudeness is a cascade, which starts with a lack reciprocity to a spontaneous social engagement that triggers an autonomic state of defense and ends with an emotional response of being offended that may lead to an aggressive reaction.
See pages: 232–234

Borderline Personality Disorder. Borderline personality disorder (BPD) is a psychiatric diagnosis including features of mood instability and difficulties in regulating emotion. From a Polyvagal perspective, the regulation of mood and emotion involves the neural regulation of the autonomic nervous system. Thus, the theory would lead to hypotheses that borderline personality distorder would be associated with a challenged social engagement system and especially the efficiency of ventral vagal pathways in downregulating sympathetic activation. This hypothesis has been tested and supported (Austin, Riniolo, & Porges, 2007).
See pages: 127, 135, 149–153

Connectedness. Polyvagal Theory refers to the social connectedness that define trusting relationships that humans have with others as a biological imperative. Humans can also feel connected to their pets, which are usually other mammals with reciprocal social engagement systems.
See pages: 51, 180–182, 192, 230

Co-regulation. Within Polyvagal Theory co-regulation involves the mutual regulation of physiological state between individuals. For example, within the mother-infant dyad the mother not only is calming her infant, but the infant's response of relaxing and calming to the mother's vocalizations, facial expressions, and gestures has the reciprocal effect of calming the mother. If the mother is unsuccessful in calming her infant, the mother's physiological state also becomes dysregulated. Co-regulation can also extend to groups such as families. For example, following the death of a family member, frequently the presence of others support the biobehavoral state of grieving person.
See pages: 48-51, 80, 118-120, 195

Cranial nerves. Cranial nerves emerge directly from the brain, in contrast to spinal nerves that emerge from segments of the spinal cord. Cranial nerves are functionally conduits that contain both motor and sensory pathways. Humans have twelve pairs of cranial nerves (I–XII). They are: the olfactory nerve (I), the optic nerve (II), oculomotor nerve (III), trochlear nerve (IV), trigeminal nerve (V), abducens nerve (VI), facial nerve (VII), vestibulocochlear nerve (VIII), glossopharyngeal nerve (IX), vagus nerve (X), accessory nerve (XI), and hypoglossal nerve (XII). Other than the vagus, which provides pathways

for both sensory and motor communication with several visceral organs, cranial nerves primarily relay information to and from regions of the head and neck.
See pages: 134–135

Cybernetics. MIT mathematician Norbert Wiener (1948) coined the term cybernetics to define a science of control and communication in animals and machines. Polyvagal Theory uses concepts from cybernetics to emphasize the feedback loops within the body and between individuals that regulate physiological state.
Similar concepts discussed throughout.

Death feigning/shutdown system. In mammals under certain conditions the nervous system reverts to a primitive defense response characterized by appearing to be inanimate. This defense pattern is frequently observed in vertebrates, such as reptiles and amphibians, that evolved prior to the phylogenetic emergence of mammals. However, mammals are great consumers of oxygen and the immobilization required in feigning death is associated with a decrease in the capacity to oxygenate the blood and an inability to deliver sufficient oxygenated blood to the brain to support consciousness. This massive depression of autonomic function is due to activation of the dorsal vagal circuit, which depresses respiration (apnea) and slows heart rate (bradycardia). Polyvagal Theory proposes that death feigning is an adaptive response to life threat when options for fight/flight behaviors are minimized, such as during restraint or when there is an inability to escape. During conditions of life threat, the nervous system through neuroception may revert to the ancient immobilization defense system. Polyvagal Theory emphasizes aspects of this life threat response in understanding trauma reactions. The theory functionally operationalizes a trauma response as the body's physiological response to life threat that would include features of death feigning such as fainting (vasovagal syncope), defecation, and dissociation.

See pages: 50, 55, 61, 103, 131

Depression. Depression is a common and serious mood disorder that influences feelings, thoughts, and behavior. Polyvagal Theory assumes that depression has a physiological state profile that could be explained by the Polyvagal Theory. Hypothetically, the profile would include a down regulation of the social engagement system and atypical coordination between sympathetic and dorsal vagal pathways. The latter point may lead to behavior oscillating between high levels of motor activity coincident with sympathetic activation and lethargy coincident with depressed sympathetic activity and increased dorsal vagal activity.

See pages: 75, 135, 138, 153, 200, 206

Dissociation. Dissociation is a process of losing a sense of presence resulting in experiencing a disconnection and a lack of continuity between thoughts, memories, surroundings, and actions. For many people dissociation is within the range of normal psychological experiences and is manifested as daydreaming. For others dissociation is sufficiently disruptive that it results in a loss of personal identity and creates severe difficulties in relationships and in functioning in everyday life. Trauma history is frequently associated with the severe disruptive effects of dissociation and may result in a psychiatric diagnosis.

Polyvagal Theory interprets dissociation in response to life threat as a component of an immobilization or death feigning defense response. Polyvagal Theory interprets dissociation as an adaptive reaction to life threat challenges, which unlike the effects of a prolonged death feigning response would not compromise the neurobiological needs for oxygen and blood flow. Based on Polyvagal Theory, one could speculate that there may be gradations in reactions to life threat from total shutdown and collapse mimicking the death feigning responses of small mammals to an immobilization of the body during which muscles lose tension and the mind dissociates from the physical event.
See pages: 54-55, 62, 161-162, 168, 174, 176, 200, 235

Dissolution. Dissolution is a construct introduced by the philosopher Herbert Spencer (1820–1903) to describe evolution in reverse. It was adapted by John Hughlings Jackson (1835–1911) to describe how brain damage and brain disease function similarly to a process of "de-evolution" in which evolutionarily older circuits become disinhibited (Jackson, 1884). Polyvagal Theory adapts dissolution to explain the phylogenetically ordered hierarchy in which the autonomic nervous system responds with progressively evolutionarily older circuits.
See pages: 64, 172; see **phylogenetically order hierarchy**

Dorsal vagal complex. The dorsal vagal complex is located in the brainstem and consists primarily of two nuclei, the dorsal nucleus of the vagus and the nucleus of the solitary tract. This area integrates and coordinates sensory information from visceral organs via sensory pathways in the vagus that terminate in the nucleus of the solitary track with the motor outflow originating in the dorsal nucleus of the vagus that terminate

on visceral organs. Both the nucleus of the solitary tract and the dorsal nucleus of the vagus have a viscerotopic organization in which specific areas of each nucleus are associated with specific visceral organs. The motor pathways from this nucleus provide the unmyelinated vagal pathways that travel through the vagus and primarily terminate in subdiaphragmatic organs. Note that a few of the unmyelinated vagal pathways may also terminate on supradiaphragmatic organs such as the heart and bronchi. This is the likely mechanism for bradycardia in preterm infants and is potentially related to asthma. The vagal pathways originating in the dorsal nucleus of the vagus have been referred to in various publications as the dorsal vagus, the subdiaphragmatic vagus, the unmyelinated vagus, and the vegetative vagus.
See pages: 111, 133, 173, 226, 243

Efferent nerves. Efferent nerves are the neural pathways that send information from the central nervous system (i.e., brain and spinal cord) to a target organ. They are also called motor fibers because they send signals to organs that influence how the organs function.
See: throughout

Enteric nervous system. The enteric nervous system consists of a mesh-like system of neurons that governs the function of the gastrointestinal system. The enteric nervous system is embedded in the lining of the gastrointestinal system, beginning in the esophagus and extending down to the anus. The enteric nervous system is capable of autonomous functions, although it receives considerable innervation from the autonomic nervous system. Polyvagal Theory assumes that optimal function-

ing of the enteric nervous system is dependent on the ventral vagal circuit (see ventral vagal complex) being activated by the dorsal vagal circuit (see dorsal vagal complex) not being recruited in defense, which occurs when the ventral vagal circuit is activated.
See pages: 110–111, 132, 159

Fight/flight defense system. Fight and flight behaviors are the predominant mobilized defense behaviors of mammals. Activation of the sympathetic nervous system is necessary to support the metabolic demands required to flee or fight. Withdrawal from the ventral vagal circuit and a dampening of the integrated social engagement system facilitate efficient and effective activation of the sympathetic nervous system in supporting the metabolic demands for fight and flight behaviors.
See pages: 50, 54-56, 61, 66-69, 72, 80-84, 101-103, 108, 111-112, 128-129, 137–138, 144, 156-157, 171–173, 174, 178, 194, 199, 202, 224-229, 234, 236, 243

Heart rate variability. Heart rate variability reflects the variation in the time between heartbeats. A healthy heart does not beat with a constant rate. Only a heart without neural innervation would beat at a relatively constant rate. Much of the variability in heart rate is determined by vagal influences especially through the myelinated ventral vagus (see ventral vagal complex), which is manifested in respiratory sinus arrhythmia (see respiratory sinus arrhythmia). Other contributions to heart rate variability may come through the dorsal vagus. Blocking vagal influences to the heart with atropine will remove virtually all heart rate variability.
See pages: 36-42, 59, 97-98, 106, 144

Homeostasis. Homeostasis reflects the neural and neurochemical processes through which our body regulates visceral organs to optimize health, growth, and restoration. Although the word is derived from the Greek word meaning same or steady, homeostasis is better understood as the product of a negative feedback system that oscillates around a "set" point. In some physiological systems, greater amplitude of the oscillations (i.e., rhythmic deviations from the set point) is a positive indicator of health (e.g., respiratory sinus arrhythmia), and in other situations it is a negative indicator of health (e.g., blood pressure variability). Oscillations in physiological systems are primarily a reflection of neural and neurochemical feedback mechanisms.
See pages: 62, 132, 158, 173

Interoception. Interoception is the process describing both conscious feelings and unconscious monitoring of bodily processes by the nervous system. Interoception, similar to other sensory systems, has four components: 1) Sensors located in internal organs to evaluate internal conditions; 2) Sensory pathways conveying information from the organs to the brain; 3) Brain structures to interpret sensory information and to regulate the organs response to the changing internal conditions; and 4) Motor pathways that communicate information from the brain to the organs and to change the state of the organs. In Polyvagal Theory interoception is the process providing the signal to the brain of changes in physiological state (see Porges, 1993). In contexts in which there are cues of risk or safety, interoception would occur after the process of neuroception. Interoception may result in a conscious awareness of a bodily response. In contrast, neuroception occurs outside conscious awareness.
See pages: 142–143

Listening. Listening is an active process to understand the acoustic information being presented. In contrast to listening, hearing is the detection of acoustic information. Polyvagal Theory emphasizes the role of middle ear structures in enhancing the ability to listen and understand human voice.
See pages: 48–49, 71–72, 75, 87–96, 100, 103, 108–109, 114–116, 118, 134, 170, 186, 189, 191

Listening Project Protocol. The Listening Project Protocol (LPP) is a listening intervention designed to reduce auditory hypersensitivities, improve auditory processing, calm physiological state, and support spontaneous social engagement. The intervention is currently known as the *Safe and Sound Protocol* (SSP). The SSP is available to professionals only through Integrated Listening Systems (http://integratedlistening.com/ssp-safe-sound-protocol/).

The LPP/SSP is a theoretical departure from the disciplines frequently involved in the treatment of auditory processing disorders, which emphasize the role of central structures in the processing of speech. LPP/SSP was theoretically designed to reduce auditory hypersensitivities by recruiting the anti-masking functions of the middle ear muscles to optimize the transfer function of the middle ear for the processing of human speech. LPP/SSP is based on an "exercise" model that uses computer altered acoustic stimulation to modulate the frequency band passed to the participant. The frequency characteristics of the acoustic stimulation are theoretically selected based on the documented frequency band and weights associated with contemporary techniques used to extract human voice from background sounds. During normal listening to human speech, via descending central mechanisms, the middle ear muscles contract and stiffen the ossicular chain. This process changes the middle ear transfer function and effectively removes most of the "masking" low frequency background sounds from the acoustic environment and allows human voice to be more effectively processed by higher brain structures. Modulation of the acoustic energy within the frequencies of human voice, similar to exaggerated vocal prosody, is hypothesized to recruit and modulate the neural regulation of the middle ear muscles, functionally reduce auditory hypersensitivities, stimulate spontaneous social engagement, and calm physiological state by increasing the influence of ventral vagal pathways on the heart.

Theoretically, the vocal music has been processed to "exercise" the neural regulation of the middle ear muscles to improve the auditory processing of human vocalizations. The acoustic stimuli, which represent the range of normal human speech, are modulated and presented to both ears. The intervention stimuli are delivered through headphones. The protocol consists of 60 minutes of listening on five sequential days and is delivered via a MP3 or iPod device in a quiet room without major distractors, while the clinician, parent, or researcher provide social support to insure that the participant remains calm. For additional information see Porges et al. (2013, 2014) and Porges & Lewis (2010).

See pages: 87-96, 114-116, 208, 211

Middle ear muscles. The two smallest striated muscles in the body, the tensor tympani and the stapedius, are located in the middle ear. The middle ear is the portion of the auditory system between the eardrum and the cochlea (inner ear). Middle ear structures include the ossicles and the muscles regulating the stiffness of the ossicle chain. When these muscles are tense, they stiffen the ossicle chain and increase the tension of the eardrum.

This process changes the characteristics of sound that reaches the inner ear. The inner ear transduces sound into a neural code that is transmitted to the brain. The tensing of the middle ear muscles reduces the influence of low-frequency sounds and functionally improves the ability to process the human voice. The middle ear muscles are regulated by special visceral efferent pathways (see Figure 1 and special viceral efferent pathways).
See pages: 76–79, 87–89, 91, 94-95, 109, 114-117, 137–138, 186, 207

Middle ear transfer function. As middle ear muscle tone changes there is a change in the transfer of acoustic energy through the middle ear structures to the inner ear. Borg and Counter (1989) described a role of the middle ear muscles in facilitating the extraction of human speech by dampening the transmission of low frequency noise from the external environment to the inner ear. The Borg and Counter model explains why auditory hypersensitivity is a symptom of Bell's palsy, a condition characterized by a lateralized paralysis of the facial nerve including the pathway regulating the stapedius muscle in the middle ear. Borg and Counter (1989) provide a scientific basis to investigate whether improvements in auditory processing would occur if neural regulation of the middle ear muscles were rehabilitated through the exercises embedded in LPP/SSP (see Listening Project Protocol). The extrapolation from normalizing the middle ear transfer function to improved vagal regulation of the heart is based on the theoretical model elaborated in Porges and Lewis (2010) and linked to the social engagement system described in the Polyvagal Theory (Porges, 2011).
See pages: 88–89, 115–116

Neural expectancy. Within Polyvagal Theory, neural expectancy refers to the predisposition wired into our nervous system that anticipates a reciprocal response to a spontaneous social engagement behavior. Neural expectancies promote social interactions, bonding, and trust. When neural expectancies are met calm states are supported, while violations of these expectancies may trigger physiological states of defense.
See: play and **neural exercise**

Neural exercise. Polyvagal Theory focuses on specific neural exercises that provide opportunities to optimize the regulation of physiological state. According to the theory, neural exercises consisting of transitory disruptions and repairs of physiological state through social interactions would promote greater resilience. Play, such as peek-a-boo, is an example of a neural exercise that parents frequently employ with their children.
See pages: 45, 80, 82–84, 91, 118, 121, 155–156, 187, 191, 208

Neuroception. Neuroception is the process through which the nervous system evaluates risk without requiring awareness. This automatic process involves brain areas that evaluate cues of safety, danger, and life threat. Once these are detected via neuroception, physiological state automatically shifts to optimize survival. Although we are usually not aware of cues that trigger neuroception, we tend to be aware of the physiological shift (i.e., interoception). Sometimes we experience this as feelings in our gut or heart or as an intuition that the context is dangerous. Alternatively, this system also triggers physiological

states that support trust, social engagement behaviors, and the building of strong relationships. Neuroception is not always accurate. Faulty neuroception might detect risk when there is no risk or identify cues of safety when there is risk.
See pages: 43, 65–73, 83-87, 91-94, 107, 113, 143, 147-150, 153, 171, 175, 177-178, 186, 197, 230, 238

Nucleus ambiguus. The nucleus ambiguus is located in the brainstem ventral to the dorsal motor nucleus of the vagus. Cells in the nucleus ambiguus contain motor neurons associated with three cranial nerves (glossopharyngeal, vagus, and accessory), which control striated muscles of pharynx, larynx, esophagus, and neck through somatomotor pathways and the bronchi and heart through myelinated ventral vagal pathways.
See pages: 111, 133, 170

Nucleus of the solitary track. The nucleus of the solitary track is located in the brainstem and serves as the primary sensory nucleus of the vagus.
See pages: 111, 133

Oxytocin. Oxytocin is a mammalian hormone that also acts as a neurotransmitter in the brain. Oxytocin is primarily produced within the brain and released by the pituitary gland. In women oxytocin acts to regulate reproductive functions including childbirth and breast-feeding. However, oxytocin is released in both sexes. In the brain, oxytocin is involved in social cognition and social recognition. The social functions of oxytocin are related to the influence of oxytocin on the brainstem areas involved in the ventral vagal complex and the

dorsal vagal complex. Since both vagal complexes have abundant oxytocin receptors, many of the positive features attributed to oxytocin overlap with the positive features described in the Polyvagal Theory as social engagement and immobilization without fear.
See pages: 122, 139, 243

Parasympathetic nervous system. The parasympathetic nervous system is one of the two main divisions of the autonomic nervous system. The primary neural pathways of this system are vagal and primarily support health, growth, and restoration. However, Polyvagal Theory emphasizes that under certain life-threatening conditions, specific vagal pathways, which would normally support homeostasis and health, can respond defensively and inhibit health-related functions.
See pages: 58–59, 62–63, 130–131, 169, 171–172, 212, 223–225

Physiological state. See autonomic state.
See: throughout

Phylogenetically ordered hierarchy. Polyvagal Theory proposes that the components of the autonomic nervous system react to challenges following a hierarchy in which the phylogenetically newer circuits react first. This pattern of evolution in reverse is consistent with the Jacksonian principle of dissolution (see dissolution). Functionally, the order of reactivity proceeds through the following sequence: myelinated ventral vagus, sympathetic nervous system, unmyelinated dorsal vagus.
See pages: 64, 128, 225; see **dissolution**

Phylogeny. Phylogeny is the science that describes the evolutionary history of a species. As a science, it provides evolution-based methods for taxonomic grouping of organisms. Within Polyvagal Theory there is an interest in the phylogenetic transitions in autonomic function among vertebrates with a focus on the transition from primitive extinct reptiles to mammals.
See pages: 46, 61–63, 76, 82, 99, 101, 107–108, 128, 130–131, 161, 225–226, 229, 244

Play. Polyvagal Theory defines interactive play as a "neural exercise" that enhances the co-regulation of physiological state to promote the neural mechanisms involved in supporting mental and physical health. Interactive play as a neural exercise requires synchronous and reciprocal behaviors between individuals and necessitates an awareness of each other's social engagement system. Access to the social engagement system insures that the sympathetic activation involved in the mobilization does not hijack the nervous system, resulting in playful movements transitioning into aggressive behavior.
See pages: 61, 80-83, 129, 154-157, 243-244

Post-Traumatic Stress Disorder (PTSD). PTSD is a psychiatric diagnosis reflecting the consequences of experiencing a traumatic event such as sexual assault, severe injury, war, earthquake, hurricane, or a bad accident. Polyvagal Theory focuses on the response to the event and not the qualities of the event. This focus on the response is consistent with the observation that there are great variations in individual reactions to a common 'traumatic' event. A common 'traumatic' event may be devastating to an individual and disrupt their life, while others may be more resilient and less affected. Because of the range of reactivity and recovery trajec-

tories, Polyvagal Theory focuses on the profile of the reaction to infer shifts in neural regulation of autonomic state and emphasizes the mediated via dorsal vagal pathways life threat response. Based on Polyvagal Theory, many of the problems associated with PTSD are emergent features following a life threat response that are manifested as a dysfunctional social engagement system and a low threshold for either the sympathetic nervous system or the dorsal vagal circuit to respond in defense.
See pages: 56, 70, 76, 79-80, 85, 90, 165, 202

Prosody. Prosody is the intonation in voice that conveys emotion. Polyvagal Theory emphasizes that prosody is mediated by vagal mechanisms and, similar to heart rate variability (i.e., respiratory sinus arrhythmia), conveys information about physiological state.
See pages: 50, 64-65, 75, 91-92, 104, 109, 114, 134, 137, 139-140, 143, 147, 186

Respiratory sinus arrhythmia. Respiratory sinus arrhythmia (RSA) is characterized by rhythmic increases and decreases in heart rate occurring at the frequency of spontaneous breathing. The amplitude of this periodic heart rate process is a valid index of the influence of the ventral vagus on the heart (see Lewis et. al. 2012).
See pages: 38, 41, 59–60, 87, 98, 144

Safety. Polyvagal Theory proposes a neurophysiological model of safety and trust. The model emphasizes that safety is defined by feeling safe and not by the removal of threat. Feeling safe is dependent on three conditions: 1) the autonomic nervous system cannot be in a state that supports defense; 2) the social engagement system needs to be activated to down regulate sympathetic activation and functionally contain the sympathetic nervous system and the dorsal vagal circuit within an optimal range (homeostasis) that would support health, growth, and restoration; and 3) to detect cues of safety (e.g., prosodic vocalizations, positive facial expressions and gestures) via neuroception. In everyday situations, the cues of safety may initiate the sequence by triggering the social engagement system via the process of neuroception, which will contain autonomic state within a homeostatic range and restrict the autonomic nervous system from reacting in defense. This constrained range of autonomic state has been referred to as the window of tolerance (see Ogden et. al. 2006; Siegel, 1999) and can be expanded through neural exercises embedded in therapy. **See:** throughout

Safety in therapeutic settings. From a Polyvagal perspective feeling safe is an important moderator influencing the effectiveness of many therapeutic manipulations including medical procedures, psychotherapy, and psychoeducation. The theory assumes that physiological (autonomic) state functions as an intervening variable influencing the effectiveness of treatment. More specifically the theory assumes that for treatments to be effective and efficient it is necessary to keep the autonomic nervous system out of states of defense. Activating the social engagement system with its ventral vagal pathways (see ventral vagal complex) enable the autonomic nervous system to support health, growth, and restoration. In this state of safety, the autonomic nervous system is not easily recruited in defense. Note that this principle of 'feeling safe' as the precursor of treatment is not well integrated into educational, medical, and mental health treatment models. In addition, the physical environments in which therapy is delivered are seldom vetted for cues (e.g., low frequency background

sounds, street noises, ventilation system sounds, vibrations from elevators and escalators) that would trigger, via neuroception, defensive states of the autonomic nervous system, which would interfere with the effectiveness of the treatment.
See pages: 86, 94, 202, 222, 231, 237, 242

Self-regulation. Self-regulation is a term frequently used to describe an individual's ability to regulate their own behavior without the aid of another person. Self-regulation is often a defining feature of a child's ability to deal in the classroom or in a novel situation. Polyvagal Theory does not treat self-regulation as a learned skill, but interprets self-regulation skills as a product of the nervous system that can maintain feelings of safety in the absence of receiving cues of safety from another person. The theory emphasizes that through processes of co-regulation, an individual develops a capacity to self-regulate. The theory emphasizes that the mutual, synchronous, and reciprocal interactions between individuals that define co-regulation function as a neural exercise enhancing the ability to self-regulate in the absence of opportunities to co-regulate.
See pages: 97-125

Singing. Polvagal Theory interprets singing as a neural exercise of the social engagement system. Singing requires slow exhalations, while controlling the muscles of the face and head to produce the modulated vocalizations that we recognize as vocal music. The slow exhalations calm autonomic state by increasing the impact of ventral vagal pathways on the heart. During the exhalation phase of breathing, vagal motor fibers send an inhibitory signal (i.e., vagal brake) to the heart's pacemaker that slows heart rate. During the inhalation phase of breath-

ing the vagal influence to the heart is diminished and heart rate increases. Singing requires longer exhalations relative to inhalations, which promotes a vagal mediated calm physiological state. The process of singing couples the exercise of turning on and off the 'vagal brake' with the exercise of the neural regulation of the muscles of the face and head, including facial muscles, middle ear muscles for listening, and muscles of the larynx and pharynx for vocal intonation. Thus, singing provides an opportunity to exercise the entire integrated social engagement system. Chants, oral readings, and playing a musical instrument would also provide opportunities to exercise the system.
See pages: 71, 92–93, 117-118, 185–186, 189

Single trial learning. Single trial learning is a specific type of learning which occurs in a single pairing of a response and stimulus and is not strengthened over time by repeated exposures. Polyvagal Theory proposes that most cases of single trial learning occur when the response includes features of the dorsal vagal circuit. Moreover, Polyvagal Theory suggests that the profound shutdown reactions to life threat, which are often antecedent to PTSD, are a manifestation of single trial learning. Thus, single trial learning paradigms in which the conditioned responses include defecation, death feigning, fainting, and nausea may provide insights into the treatment of survivors of trauma.
See pages: 162–167

Social engagement system. As illustrated in Figure 1, the social engagement system consists of a somatomotor component and a visceromotor component. The somatomotor component involves special visceral efferent pathways (see special visceral

efferent pathways) that regulate the striated muscles of the face and head. The visceromotor component involves the myelinated supradiaphragmatic vagus that regulates the heart and bronchi. Functionally, the social engagement system emerges from a heart–face connection that coordinates the heart with the muscles of the face and head. The initial function of the system is to coordinate sucking-swallowing-breathing-vocalizing. Atypical coordination of this system early in life is an indicator of subsequent difficulties in social behavior and emotional regulation.
See pages: 47-51, 68-69, 72–73, 76-77, 80-87, 91–92, 96, 111-123, 129, 138, 147, 151, 157, 166, 175, 185–186, 188, 190, 194, 210, 234-236, 242–243

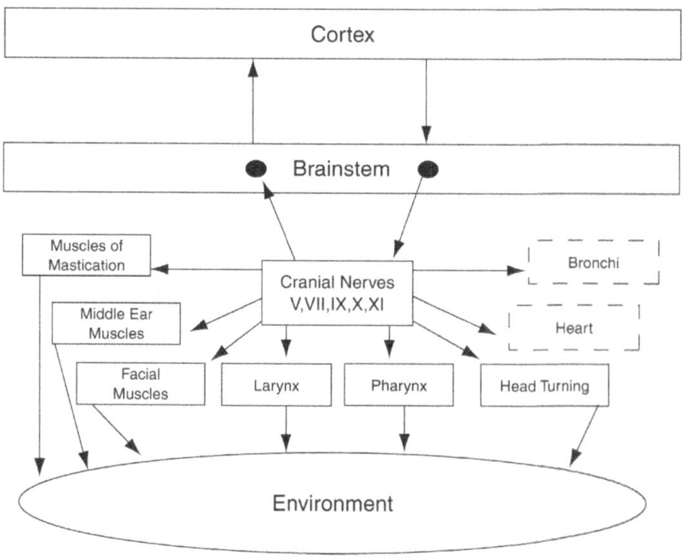

Figure 1 The Social Engagement System
The social engagement system consists of a somatomotor component (solid blocks) and a visceromotor component (dashed blocks). The somatomotor component involves special visceral efferent pathways that regulate the striated muscles of the face and head, while the visceromotor component involves the myelinated vagus that regulates the heart and bronchi.

Somatomotor. Somatomotor pathways are motor pathways regulating striated muscle. The pathways regulating the striated muslces of the face and head travel through cranial nerves and those regulating the muscles of the limbs and trunk travel through spinal nerves.
See: social engagement system

Special visceral efferent pathways. Special visceral efferent fibers originate from motor nuclei in the brainstem (ambiguus, facial, and trigeminal) that develop from the branchiomotor column (i.e., ancient gill arches) of the embryo and innervate striated muscle fibers (muscles of mastication involved in ingestion, facial musculature involved in emotional expression, muscles of the pharynx and larynx involved in vocalizations, and muscles of the middle ear involved in listening) associated with the pharyngeal arches. Special visceral efferent pathways compose the somatomotor component of the social engagement system (see Figure 1).
See: social engagement system

Subdiaphragmatic vagus. The subdiaphragmatic vagus is the branch of the vagus that connects brainstem areas with organs located below the diaphragm. The motor fibers in this branch of the vagus originate primarily in the dorsal nucleus of the vagus. These motor fibers are predominantly unmyelinated.
See pages: 111, 132, 158–163, 167, 170, 172–174, 226

Supradiapragmatic vagus. The supradiaphragmatic vagus is the branch of the vagus that connects brainstem areas with organs (e.g. bronchi, heart) located above the diaphragm (see Figure 1). The motor fibers in this branch of the vagus originate primarily in the nucleus ambiguus, the source nucleus in

the brainstem for the ventral vagus. These motor fibers are predominantly myelinated.
See pages: 110, 132, 162, 173-174

Sympathetic nervous system. The sympathetic nervous system is one of the two main divisions of the autonomic nervous system. The sympathetic nervous system functions to increase blood flow throughout the body to support movement. Polyvagal Theory focuses on the role that sympathetic nervous system has in increasing cardiac output to support movement and fight-flight behaviors.
See pages: 51, 54–55, 58–59, 63, 69, 80, 82–83, 101–105, 108, 111–112, 128–132, 138, 145-146, 157, 160–161, 171–174, 185, 194, 199, 212, 223-228, 236

Taste aversion. Taste aversion is an example of single trial learning (see single trial learning). Generally, taste aversion develops after ingestion of a food that causes nausea or vomiting. Patients receiving nausea inducing chemotherapy have been found to develop aversions to normal dietary items consumed in close temporal relation to treatment administrations. Polyvagal Theory proposes that the neural process underlying the perseverance of taste aversion may lead to a better understanding on how trauma gets encoded in the nervous system and why trauma is difficult to treat.
See pages: 162, 167

Vagal afferents. Approximately 80 percent of the neural fibers in the vagus are afferent (sensory). Most vagal sensory fibers travel from the internal organs to an area of the brainstem known as the nucleus of the solitary track. Of note, medical

training provides a very limited understanding of vagal afferents. Thus, medical treatments seldom acknowledge possible influences due to feedback from the treated organ to the brain. Changing sensory feedback has the potential to influence mental and physical health.
See pages: 110, 204, 212

Vagal brake. The vagal brake reflects the inhibitory influence of vagal pathways on the heart, which slow the intrinsic rate of the heart's pacemaker. If the vagus no longer influences the heart, heart rate spontaneously increases without any change in sympathetic excitation. The intrinsic heart rate of young healthy adults is about 90 beats per minute. However, baseline heart rate is noticeably slower due to the influence of the vagus functioning as a "vagal brake." The vagal brake represents the actions of engaging and disengaging the vagal influences to the heart's pacemaker. It has been assumed that the vagal brake is mediated through the myelinated ventral vagus. Although the unmyelinated vagal fibers appear to mediate clinical bradycardia in preterm neonates, this process has not been conceptualized in the vagal brake construct. Thus, discussing clinical bradycardia as a product of a vagal brake should be clarified by emphasizing that it is through a vagal mechanism different from the protective ventral vagal influence.
See pages: 57–68, 111, 146, 149

Vagal paradox. Vagal influences to visceral organs have been assumed to be protective. However, vagal influences can be lethal by stopping the heart or disruptive by triggering fainting or defecation. These responses, often linked to fear, are mediated by the vagus. The vagal paradox was initially observed in research with preterm infants in which respiratory sinus arrhythmia was

protective and bradycardia was potentially lethal. This created a paradox, since both respiratory sinus arrhythmia and bradycardia were both mediated by vagal mechanisms. The contradiction was solved by the introduction of the Polyvagal Theory, which linked these responses to different vagal pathways.
See pages: 57, 60, 106–107, 130–131, 163

Vagal tone. The construct of vagal tone, or more accurately cardiac vagal tone, is usually associated with the more tonic influence of the myelinated ventral vagal pathways on the heart and is frequently indexed by the amplitude of respiratory sinus arrhythmia.
See pages: 38-39, 58-59, 143-145, 157, 174

Vagus. The vagus is the tenth cranial nerve. The vagus is the primary nerve in the parasympathetic division of the autonomic nervous system. The vagus functions as a conduit containing motor pathways originating in nucleus ambiguus and the dorsal nucleus of the vagus and sensory fibers terminating in the nucleus of the solitary tract. The vagus connects brainstem areas with structures throughout the body including the neck, thorax, and abdomen. Polyvagal Theory emphasizes the phylogenetic changes in the autonomic nervous system in vertebrates and focuses on the unique change in the vagal motor pathways that occurred with the emergence of mammals.
See: throughout

Vegetative vagus. See dorsal vagal complex.
See pages: 130, 132

Ventral vagal complex. The ventral vagal complex is an area of the brainstem involved in the regulation of the heart, bron-

chi, and the striated muscles of the face and head (see Figure 1). Specifically, this complex consists of nucleus ambiguus and the nuclei of the trigeminal and facial nerves regulating the heart and bronchi through visceromotor pathways and the muscles of mastication, middle ear, face, larynx, pharynx, and neck through special visceral efferent pathways.
See: social engagement system

Visceromotor. Visceromotor nerves are motor nerves, within the autonomic nervous system, that regulate smooth and cardiac muscles and glands.
See: social engagement system

Yoga and the social engagement system. Polyvagal Theory deconstructs yoga practices involving breath into specific neural exercises of the vagal brake (see vagal brake). Pranayama yoga is functionally a yoga of the social engagement system, since it involves neural exercises of both breath and the striated muscles of the face and head (see Figure 1).
See pages: 118

1

THE NEUROBIOLOGY OF FEELING SAFE

THOUGHTS AND FEELINGS: REFLECTIONS OF THE BRAIN AND BODY

The important role of "safety" in our life is so intuitive and so relevant that it is surprising that our institutions neglect it. Perhaps our misunderstanding of the role of safety is based on an assumption that we think we know what safety means. This assumption needs to be challenged, because there may be an inconsistency between the words we use to describe safety and our bodily feelings of safety. In the Western world, we tend to place higher value on thoughts than on feelings. Parenting and educational strategies are targeted toward expanding and enhancing cognitive processes while inhibiting bodily feelings and impulses to move. The result is a corticocentric orientation in which there is a top-down bias emphasizing mental processes and minimizing the bottom-up feeling emanating from our body. In many ways, our culture, including educational and religious institutions, has explicitly subjugated feelings of the body to the thought processes emanating from the brain. Historically, this was clearly articulated in Descartes's (1637) statement "*Je pense donc je suis*" (I think, therefore I am). Descartes did not state "*Je me sens donc je suis*" (I feel, therefore I am). Note that I used the reflexive form of the verb "to feel." In French, when "feel" is used as a reflexive verb, it emphasizes that feelings reside inside the person. However, in English, the meaning of the verb "to feel" is ambiguous, meaning either the sensory feelings associated with physically touching an object or the subjective experience associated with an emotional response.

Arguments regarding the relative contributions of cognitions and feelings have been at the core of historical questions related to how human behavior and emotional experience can be understood, modified, and optimized. Only during the past 50 years have emotion and investigation of subjective states of feeling become an accepted research domain within psychology. Prior research and its influence on educational (and parenting models) and clinical treatment models emphasized the cognitive pathway with the objective of nurturing cognitive functions and containing subjective feelings. This focus emphasized objective, measurable indices of behaviors and cognitive functions while dismissing subjective reports of feelings.

THE STUDY OF FEELINGS AS A LEGITIMATE SCIENTIFIC TOPIC

The scientific world I entered as a graduate student in 1966 did not consider the study of bodily feelings a valid research area. It was a scientific arena in which "emotion" could be discussed only in terms of motivation. Studies of emotion were primarily conducted with laboratory rats; motivation was manipulated by controlling the availability of food, while emotional reactivity was quantified by the amount the animal defecated (e.g., Hall, 1934).

It was a scientific world that preceded the resurgence of behaviorism and the interest in mental processes driven by the cognitive revolution. Behaviorism merged into applied areas as behavioral techniques were integrated into special education and clinical psychology. Cognitive science grew as new models of memory, learning, decision-making, concept formation, and problem-solving were developed and expanded into engineering and computer science, as models of artificial intelligence and machine learning were generated. As improved measurements of brain function (e.g., brain imaging and electrophysiological techniques) became available to cognitive scientists, they applied imaging and electrophysiological technologies and cognitive science merged with neuroscience (i.e., cognitive neuroscience). Although both behavior and cognition are dependent on the nervous system, neither applied behaviorism nor cognitive science incorporated an understanding of neural physiological state as a mediator of the behaviors and psychological processes under study. Behaviorism continued to be agnostic of the nervous system, while cognitive neuroscience focused on identifying measurable brain-based correlates of cognitive processes.

When I entered graduate school, I was immediately attracted to a new interdisciplinary area labeled psychophysiology. The first journal of this new discipline was published only a couple of years before I entered graduate school, and there were only two or three books on the topic that could serve as resources for graduate study. Psychophysiological research focused on measuring physiological reactions to psychological manipulations (Stern, 1964). I was attracted to the methodologies of psychophysiology, which provided an objective and quantifiable strategy, using physiological responses (e.g., electrodermal, respiration, heart rate, vasomotor), to tap into subjective experiences without requiring the subject to make a voluntary response. This correlative approach linking mental processes to neurophysiological events is still the prevalent model in psychophysiology and in cognitive neuroscience. During the past 50 years, there has been little change in this paradigm, although there have been major advances in the development of the sensors used to monitor physiology and neurophysiology and the quantitative methods applied to extract variables that track mental processes.

HEART RATE VARIABILITY IN PSYCHOPHYSIOLOGICAL RESEARCH

In graduate school, my research produced the first published studies that quantified heart rate variability both as a dependent variable (Porges & Raskin, 1969) and then as an intervening variable (Porges, 1972). The distinction between the use of heart rate variability as a dependent variable and as an intervening variable is an important defining feature in understanding a paradigm shift. At the time I started my studies, psychophysiological paradigms were defined by using physiological responses as dependent variables. This meant that physiological responses were monitored in response to a well-controlled psychological manipulation. This paradigm fit the traditional stimulus-response (S-R) model in which the psychological manipulation was the "S" and the physiological response was the "R." Within this paradigm, my research reported changes in heart rate, heart rate variability, and respiration.

My work documented that a reduction in heart rate variability was a robust indicator of sustained attention and mental effort. In conducting this research, I noticed that when participants were not engaged in an attention-demanding task, there were individual differences in heart rate variability. These baseline measures of heart rate variability were related to the magnitude of the stimulus-dependent changes in heart rate and heart rate variability. Based on this observation, I started to partition the participants into subgroups defined by high or low heart rate variability (e.g., Porges, 1972, 1973). These studies were prescient and led to an explosion in research publications linking individual differences in heart rate variability to cognitive performance, sensitivity to environmental stimuli, psychiatric diagnoses, and mental and physical fitness and resilience. As heart rate variability became established in the literature, others worked on techniques to enhance heart rate variability through biofeedback, breathing exercises, physical fitness, and meditation.

NEURAL MECHANISMS MEDIATING HEART RATE VARIABILITY

Once I observed the link between individual differences in heart rate variability and both measures of attention, such as reaction time, and measures of autonomic reactivity (e.g., heart rate changes), my research took on a new agenda. I directed my efforts toward figuring out why individual differences in heart rate variability were related to sustained attention and behavioral state regulation. This led to animal research in which I studied the neural regulation of the heart to understand the neural pathways responsible for the beat-to-beat heart rate patterns contributing to heart rate variability.

As I studied neurophysiology and neuroanatomy, I learned that buried in the literature was sufficient information to extract a neural signature of vagal regulation from heart rate variability. In a publication from the early 1900s, German physiologist H. E. Hering (1910) reported that breathing provided a functional test of the vagal control of the heart. Hering stated, "It is known with breathing that a demonstrable lowering of heart rate . . . is indicative of the function of the vagi."

DEVELOPING A SENSITIVE METRIC OF VAGAL REGULATION OF THE HEART

With the knowledge that vagal cardioinhibitory fibers fire with a breathing pattern, I had the necessary neurophysiological justification to transition from a global measure of heart rate variability to a more accurate component of heart rate variability that indexed vagal regulation of the heart. This led to the development of a method that quantified respiratory sinus arrhythmia as an accurate index of cardiac vagal tone. Respiratory sinus arrhythmia is the functional manifestation of vagal influences on heart rate as described by Hering. The breathing-related changes in vagal influence on the heart are manifested as rhythmic increases and decreases in beat-to-beat heart rate, with greater vagal influences producing greater differences in the rhythmic increases and decreases. Respiratory sinus arrhythmia is a functional index of a neural feedback loop that dynamically adjusts the inhibitory influence of the vagus on the heart's pacemaker. The feedback system has inputs from the lungs and heart going up to the brainstem and also projections from higher brain areas down to the brainstem. The output parameters of the feedback system provide measures of amplitude and frequency. The amplitude is a manifestation of vagal influence, and the periodicity reflects respiration rate.

With this new tool, my research transitioned from a correlative approach to a neurophysiologically informed model that could continuously monitor the neural regulation of autonomic state via the vagus. With this new technology, I could accurately monitor the specific state changes in vagal regulation. By the mid-1980s, my research had shifted to studies of clinical populations that had behavioral state regulation disorders, such as preterm infants. Since my research was now focusing on monitoring physiological state, I wanted to expand to clinical environments and developed a portable "vagal tone monitor" (Porges, 1985) that could monitor in hospital settings continuous values of vagal regulation of the heart. About 100 of these devices were manufactured and sold to researchers through a small company, Delta-Biometrics, which no longer exists.

INTEGRATING MEASURES OF PHYSIOLOGICAL STATE INTO S-R MODELS

From my perspective, the role of biology in both applied behavioral techniques (e.g., behavior modification) and the cognitive sciences is either lacking or underdeveloped. The integration of cognitive sciences with neural sciences did not change the model of cognitive science; it only changed dependent variables to include measures of central nervous system function. Thus, although there was a proliferation of studies imaging brain function and monitoring electrophysiology from the brain, there was no shift in paradigm. These studies maintained the historic S-R model and only marginally integrated into their model information regarding physiology or neurophysiology.

In the world of applied behavioral science, as characterized by the membership and journals of the Association of Behavioral Analysis International (ABAI), the underlying physiological state of the subject is not assumed to be a major determinant of the S-R relationships that their methods attempt to establish and strengthen. A few years ago, I was honored to give a B. F. Skinner lecture at an annual ABAI meeting. The title of my talk was "Behavior Modification Through the Lens of the Polyvagal Theory." The talk described my personal search for variables that could measure physiological state as an intervening variable between the stimulus-response (S-R) relationship that defines behavioral methods. My talk reintroduced a much older model for learning that acknowledged the important role of variations in the organism as a mediator of S-R relationships. In the S-O-R model (e.g., Woodworth, 1929), "O" represents the organism and serves as an intervening variable in S-R paradigms. However, historically the "O" in S-O-R models did not have a neurophysiological basis and did not use physiological state as a defining feature.

My talk explained that measurement of the neural regulation of the autonomic nervous system, using measures like heart rate variability, provided an opportunity to monitor the "O" that would function as an intervening variable in paradigms and protocols designed to modify behavior. In addition, I proposed that, since physiological state can be manipulated, context and other intervention features could influence the "O" to enhance outcomes. I suggested that respiratory sinus arrhythmia, as an index of vagal regulation of the heart, be used as an intervening variable in behavior modification paradigms.

I asked whether physiological state would account for individual differences and situational variations in the effectiveness of behavior modification procedures. I suggested that new behavioral paradigms be designed within the S-O-R framework. These new frameworks would use context to manipulate physiological state toward a more optimal level of vagal regulation to functionally mediate the effectiveness of behavior modification protocols. The talk was well received and provided the attendees, who all had strong behavioral perspectives, an opportunity to incorporate a neurophysiological perspective without conflicting with their methodologies and paradigms.

THE SEARCH FOR AN INTERVENING VARIABLE

My scientific journey has been a personal quest for an intervening variable that would contribute to our understanding of individual differences in behavior. This journey led me to an understanding of the importance of autonomic state as a neural platform for behavior and psychological experiences, including feelings of being safe. Basically, autonomic state influence on behavior is not causal in a one-to-one manner. However, the range of emergent behavior and psychological experience is limited by autonomic state. An alternative way of viewing this relationship is to conceptualize autonomic state changes as producing shifts in the probability (and possibility) that specific behaviors and psychological feelings will occur.

My journey, which led to the conceptualization of the Polyvagal Theory, actually maps into the pragmatic demands of the academic institutions in which I was affiliated. Universities are not structured to make faculty feel safe and secure. Universities function consistently with a clear and objective evaluative model in which ideas and papers are continuously scrutinized. Evaluative models, when chronic, shift physiological state to support defense. The physiological states that support defense are incompatible with those that support creativity and expansive theories. The academic environment has implicit rules, and understanding these rules has enabled me to be creative and to generate new perspectives.

In retrospect, I see my academic career as having three phases. The first phase was characterized by descriptive research to obtain tenure and promotion to associate professor. During this phase, I identified heart rate variability as an important phenomenon and conducted a series of empirical studies. The second phase was characterized by research on explaining the neurophysiological mechanisms mediating heart rate variability. This phase provided the scientific contributions necessary for my promotion to professor. Being a professor provided me the opportunity to apply the knowledge gained from earlier research to clinical problems. The third phase was characterized by generating the Polyvagal Theory as a basis for a brain–body or mind–body science informed by neurophysiology, neuroanatomy, and evolution. Presenting a paradigm-challenging theory is risky and, if done prematurely, can be career ending. However, it was possible for me to leverage my academic accomplishments to provide the scientific credibility necessary to present the Polyvagal Theory. For me, the third phase started more than 10 years after I was promoted to "full" professor when I presented the Polyvagal Theory as my presidential address to the Society for Psychophysiological Research (Porges, 1995). Fortunately, this phase has been very rewarding both within the academic community and the applied clinical world.

The Polyvagal Theory provided the vehicle for explaining the importance of physiological state as an intervening variable influencing behavior and our ability to interact with others. The theory provided an understanding of how risk and threat shift physiological state to support defense. Moreover, and perhaps most important, the theory explains how safety is not the removal of threat and that feeling safe is dependent on unique cues in the environment and in our relationships that have an active inhibition on defense circuits and promote health and feelings of love and trust (e.g., Porges, 1998).

SAFETY AND PHYSIOLOGICAL STATE

Safety is associated with different environmental features when defined by bodily responses versus cognitive evaluations. In a critical sense, when it comes to identifying safety from an adaptive survival perspective, the "wisdom" resides in our body and in the structures of our nervous system that function outside the realm of awareness. In other words, our cognitive evaluations of risk in the environment, including identifying potentially dangerous relationships, play a secondary role to our visceral reactions to people and places. Within Polyvagal Theory, the neural process that evaluates risk in the environment without awareness is called neuroception (Porges, 2003,

2004). Consistent with this theme, the debilitating effects of challenges to our mental and physical health, which are often defined as stressing and calibrated via changes in cognitive performance, are frequently less dependent on the physical features of the event than they are on our bodily responses.

When confronted with challenges, our body functions like a polygraph (i.e., lie detector). Features in the environment that may be comfortable and enjoyable to some may be unsettling and frightening to others. As responsible humans, sensitive parents, good friends, mentors, and clinicians, we need to listen to our own body's responses and respect the responses of others as we help ourselves and others navigate in an inherently dangerous world to find safe environments and trusting relationships.

The same features of our nervous system that protect us as we navigate the world at large provide us information about the state and needs of our clients. We have this exquisitely tuned capacity to derive their state and intention from the tone of their voice, their facial expressions, their gestures, and their posture. We may not have words for this information, but if we listen to the way they make us feel, it will inform our practice.

Polyvagal Theory challenges the parameters that our educational, legal, political, religious, and medical institutions use to define safety. By moving the defining features of "safety" from a structural model of the environment with fences, metal detectors, and surveillance monitoring to a visceral sensitivity model evaluating shifts in the neural regulation of autonomic state, the theory challenges our societal values regarding how people are treated. The theory forces us to question whether our society provides sufficient and appropriate opportunities to experience safe environments and trusting relationships. Once we recognize that the experiences within our societal institutions such as schools, hospitals, and churches are characterized by chronic evaluations that trigger feelings of danger and threat, we can see that these institutions can be as disruptive to health as political unrest, fiscal crisis, or war.

Polyvagal Theory provides a neurobiological narrative that focuses on the importance of "safety" and the adaptive consequences of detecting risk on physiological state, social behavior, psychological experience, and health. The Polyvagal Theory restructures clinical disorders as difficulties in neural regulation of specific circuits associated with turning off defensive strategies and enabling social engagement to spontaneously occur. This perspective departs from traditional learning models that assume that atypical behaviors are learned and can be modified through treatments informed by learning theory that focus on association, extinction, and habituation. While it doesn't preclude pharmacological interventions, it departs from several features of contemporary biological psychiatry in which pharmacological manipulations are the primary modes of treatment.

Polyvagal Theory provides the basis for a complementary model focusing on understanding and respecting physiological state as a "neural" platform on which different classes of adaptive behaviors can efficiently be expressed. For example, different physiological states would be associated with optimal social behavior and efficient defensive strategies. An understanding of the Polyvagal Theory helps the clinician become aware of the client's physiological state and to respect physiological state as a major determinant of the range of behavior that can be expressed. Moreover, the theory may lead to new treatments based on specific "neural exercises" that may be implemented to improve regulation of autonomic state.

THE ROLE OF SAFETY AND CUES OF SAFETY FOR SURVIVAL

As a function of evolution, the transition from reptiles to mammals resulted in a nervous system capable of identifying safety, especially in terms of which conspecifics were safe to be near and to touch. This adaptive skill required neural mechanisms that could turn off the well-developed defensive strategies that characterized reptiles and other more "primitive" vertebrates. This need for mammals to identify safety was driven by several biological needs. First, unlike our ancient extinct primitive reptilian ancestors from whom we evolved, all mammals at birth require care from their mothers. Second, several mammalian species, including humans, require long-term social interdependences to survive. For these mammalian species, isolation is "traumatic" and will severely compromise health. Thus, the ability to identify a safe environment and a safe conspecific is necessary for mammals to turn off defensive systems in order to parent and to express appropriate social behavior. Third, the mammalian nervous system requires safe environments to perform various biological and behavioral functions including reproduction, nursing, sleep, and digestion. This is especially needed during periods of great vulnerability, such as pregnancy and early life. Nested within this need for safety to enable specific biological functions are the expression of social behavior and the regulation of emotions.

Several specific neurophysiological changes that characterize the phylogenetic transition from the primitive extinct reptiles to mammals are related to social behavior and emotional regulation. Relevant to mental and physical health is the observation that these circuits are not accessible in dangerous and life-threatening environments and that the circuits are frequently not functioning appropriately in several mental and physical disorders. Polyvagal Theory emphasizes that the neural circuits that support social behavior and emotional regulation are available only when the nervous system deems the environment safe and that these circuits are involved in health, growth, and restoration.

Safety is critical in enabling humans to optimize their potentials along several domains. Safe states are a prerequisite not only for social behavior but also for accessing the higher brain structures that enable humans to be creative and generative. However, what are the features of our institutions, such as educational institutions, governments, and medical treatment centers, in promoting states of safety? What are the priorities of our culture and society in respecting individual needs for safety? We need to understand what features in the world disrupt our sense of safety and realize the cost to human potential of living in an unsafe world. As we understand our vulnerability to danger and life threat, we have to start respecting the importance of social behavior and the social engagement system (Porges, 2007) in dampening defensive systems that enable us to form strong social bonds, while simultaneously supporting health, growth, and restoration.

Various treatment models have been informed by Polyvagal Theory to understand bodily reactions and physiological states as a neurophysiological platform upon which they may integrate intervention techniques into an efficient therapeutic model. Polyvagal Theory respects how our psychological, physical, and behavioral responses are dependent on our physiological state. The theory emphasizes the bidirectional communication between bodily organs and the brain through the vagus and other nerves involved in the regulation of the autonomic nervous system. The theory provides a narrative to explain how evolution modified how our autonomic nervous system was regulated. As the theory developed, it became a story of how, through evolution, mammals departed from their vertebrate relatives with a new neural pathway that enabled them to signal safety and to co-regulate.

SOCIAL ENGAGEMENT AND SAFETY

From a Polyvagal perspective, the clinical interactions involving looking, listening, and witnessing illustrate relevant features of the theory: the social engagement system and the feedback from our bodily organs that contribute to the subjective feelings manifested in our mood states and emotions. The social engagement system is a functional collection of neural pathways that regulate the striated muscles of the face and head. The social engagement system projects bodily feelings and is a portal for changing bodily feelings along a continuum extending from a calm, safe state that would promote trust and love to a vulnerable state that would promote defensive reactions.

The act of looking and listening captures an important attribute of the social engagement system, since the process of looking at a person constitutes both an act of engagement and projects the bodily state of the observer. Based on the projected bodily state of the observer, the person being "looked at" will feel that the "looker" is welcoming or disinterested. Feeling and witnessing the client encompasses the therapist's bodily reaction to the client's engagement behavior and the projection of the bodily feelings embedded in the therapist's reciprocal engagement behavior.

Looking, listening, and feeling the other in the therapeutic moment is an illustration of the dynamic bidirectional communication between bodily state and emotional processes during a social interaction. For the social interaction to be mutually supportive and to enable a co-regulation of physiological state, the expressed cues from the dyad's social engagement systems need to communicate mutual safety and trust. When this occurs, the active participants, whether they are the child and the parent or an adult couple, are now safe in each other's arms. The process of obtaining the state of a shared intersubjective experience is metaphorically like entering the code into a combination lock; suddenly the tumblers fall into place and the lock opens.

The link between social engagement behaviors and physiological state is an evolutionary product of the transition from extinct primitive reptiles to mammals. As mammals evolved, modifications in neurophysiology enabled them to cue and detect the affective states of individuals within their species. This innovation provided them with abilities to signal whether they were safe to approach, to make physical contact, and to create social relationships. Alternatively, if their cues reflected aggression or defense, then the engagement could be immediately terminated without conflict or potential injury.

Through evolutionary processes, the nerves and structures that define the social engagement system and regulate facial expression, ingestion, listening, and vocalizing became integrated with a neural pathway of the autonomic nervous system that calms the heart and down-regulates defenses. The evolutionary processes that linked physiological state to the circuits that produce (e.g., facial expressions, vocalizations) and detect (e.g., sounds, tastes) features of emotion is a defining feature of mammals. Functionally, this integrated connection between bodily state and facial and vocal expressions enabled conspecifics to distinguish those expressing cues of safety from those expressing cues of danger and to feign death to appear to be inanimate when unable to fight or flee. This bidirectional system linking bodily states with facial expressions and vocalizations provided the portal for social communication that involves requests for co-regulation and mechanisms to calm and repair co-regulation following disruptions.

This integrated system involves the neural regulation of the muscles of the face and head that provide cues that the other is safe to approach. Embedded in the social engagement system is our biological quest for safety and an implicit biological imperative to connect and co-regulate our physiological state with another. How we look at each other is a critical feature of this capacity to connect. Subtle cues of understanding, of shared feelings, and of intent are conveyed. These cues, often covarying with the intonation or prosody of vocalization, are also communicating physiological state. Only when we are in a calm physiological state can we convey cues of safety to another. These opportunities to connect and co-regulate determine the success of relationships, whether describing mother–child, father–child, or other relationships. The social engagement system is not solely an expression of the individual's physiological state but may act as a portal of detection of distress or safety in others. When detecting safety, physiology calms. When detecting danger, physiology is activated for defense.

CONCLUSION

Polyvagal Theory provides an understanding that feeling safe is dependent on autonomic state and that cues of safety help calm our autonomic nervous system. The calming of physiological state promotes opportunities to create safe and trusting relationships, which in themselves expand opportunities to co-regulate behavioral and physiological state. This "circle" of regulation defines healthy relationships in which the relationship supports both mental and physical health. In this model, our bodily feelings (i.e., autonomic state) function as an intervening variable contributing to our reactions to others. When we are in a mobilized state characterized by sympathetic activation, we are "tuned" for defense and not for promoting cues of safety or for responding positively to cues of safety. However, when the autonomic state is regulated by ventral vagal pathways, our social engagement system coordinates cues of safety through voice and facial expression to down-regulate defense in ourselves and in others. The coordination between social engagement systems facilitates social connectedness. The theory provides an understanding of how treatment models not only need to respect bodily feelings but also need to support physiological states that optimize the "positive" attributes of the human experience.

Polyvagal Theory leads to an understanding that to connect and co-regulate with others is our biological imperative. We experience this imperative as an inherent quest for safety that can be reached only through successful social relationships in which we co-regulate our behavior and physiology. As we ponder the importance of feeling safe in our lives, we realize that understanding the physiological signatures of feelings and the cues that trigger feelings may guide us in improving our relationships and in providing support for our clients, family, and friends. Thus, to fulfill our biological imperative of connectedness, our personal agenda needs to be directed toward making individuals feel safe.

2

POLYVAGAL THEORY AND THE TREATMENT OF TRAUMA

Stephen W. Porges and Ruth Buczynski

TRAUMA AND THE NERVOUS SYSTEM

Dr. Buczynski: I am Dr. Ruth Buczynski, a state-certified psychologist in Connecticut and president of the National Institute for the Clinical Application of Behavioral Medicine (NICABM).

Today our guest is Dr. Stephen Porges. I think Stephen's work will create a shift in how we understand trauma and other disorders as well. When a person is in trauma, what is actually happening internally?

Dr. Porges: A major problem in understanding the neurophysiological responses to trauma is that trauma has been conceptualized as a stress-related disorder. By categorizing trauma as stress-related, important attributes that are specific to trauma are lost in the discussion of cause, mechanism, and treatment. At the foundation of this problem is a misunderstanding that the human nervous system responds to danger and life threat with a common stress reaction that is associated with the sympathetic nervous system and the HPA (hypothalamic-pituitary-adrenal) axis. Therapists as well as scientists have assumed that the human nervous system has a single defense or stress system that is related to managing "fight/flight" behaviors. Polyvagal Theory emphasizes that danger and life threat elicit different defensive response profiles. According to the theory, danger reactions are associated with the accepted notions of a stress response expressed in increases in autonomic activation through the sympathetic nervous system and the adrenals. However, Polyvagal Theory also identifies a second defense system related to life threat that is characterized by a massive down-regulation of autonomic function by an ancient pathway of the parasympathetic nervous system.

We are all familiar with the negative effects of the "classic" stress response, which interferes with the health-supporting functions of our nervous system. By disrupting the regulation of autonomic, immune, and endocrine systems, stress creates vulnerability for both mental and physical illnesses. This defense system is described in every academic psychology book and is central to discussions about the links between health and psychological experiences. This model has been described in subdisciplines such as neuroendocrinology, neuroimmunology, psychophysiology, and psychosomatic medicine. However, missing from these discussions is a description of a second defense system with features not of mobilization as manifested in fight/flight reactions, but of immobilization, behavioral shutdown, and dissociation. Although fight/flight behaviors are functionally adaptive in response to danger cues, fight/flight behaviors are less adaptive when there is an inability to escape or physically defend.

In contrast to fight/flight reactions, the response to life threat elicits a second defense system, which is expressed as immobilization and dissociation. When the body immobilizes in defense, it goes into a unique physiological state that is potentially lethal. This response is commonly observed in small mammals such as a wild house mouse when trapped by a cat. When a mouse is caught in the jaws of a cat, it looks dead, but it is not. We label this adaptive reaction by the mouse "death feigning," or pretending to be dead. However, this is not a conscious or voluntary response. It is an adaptive biological reaction to the inability to utilize fight/flight mechanisms to defend or to escape. This reflexive response is similar to a human passing out in fear.

Contributing to the difficulties in treating trauma is a lack of awareness of the full range of adaptive biological reactions to threats. Unfortunately, many dedicated clinicians working with traumatized patients are not familiar with the immobilization defense system. Tracking the scientific literature suggests that this blind spot has occurred due to the incompatibility of an immobilization defense system with the dominant theories of stress, which focus on the adrenals and the sympathetic nervous system to support mobilization defense strategies.

Polyvagal Theory emphasizes that our nervous system has more than one defense strategy and that the decision of whether we use a mobilized flight/flight or an immobilization shutdown defense strategy is not a voluntary decision. Outside the realm of conscious awareness, our nervous system is continuously evaluating risk in the environment, making judgments, and setting priorities for behaviors that are adaptive. These processes occur without our awareness and without the conscious mental processes that we attribute to the "executive" functions involved in decision-making.

For some people, specific physical characteristics of an environmental challenge will trigger a fight/flight behavior, while others may totally shut down in response to the same physical features. I want to emphasize that understanding the response, not the traumatic event, is more critical to the successful treatment of trauma.

For some people, traumatic events are just events, while for others these same events trigger life-threatening responses. Their bodies respond as if they are going to die, similar to the response of the mouse in the jaws of the cat.

Dr. Buczynski: Would this explain why troops of soldiers can go to war and endure horrific events, and some will get PTSD and some won't?

Dr. Porges: Yes. The problem, again, is that when we discuss a specific psychiatric disorder, we are describing a variety of symptoms that don't always cluster together. It is like a restaurant menu in which a limited selection of foods defines a lunch or a dinner. Some may enjoy the selected foods, others may find the same foods disgusting. When a clinician arrives at a diagnosis based on a collection of features, it doesn't mean that everyone with that diagnosis has experienced the same underlying neural physiological reactions or will have the same clinical manifestations.

Most clinicians understand this. They know that when a client has a specific diagnosis, it doesn't mean that they are going to be similar to any other patient that they have seen, or that the treatment that has been effective with one person will be effective with another.

ORIGINS OF THE POLYVAGAL THEORY: THE VAGAL PARADOX

Dr. Buczynski: So let's get into Polyvagal Theory and how that sheds light on our understanding of trauma.

Dr. Porges: Before I discuss the Polyvagal Theory, I would like to give a little background about why there is a Polyvagal Theory.

I frequently say that I never was looking for a Polyvagal Theory. My academic life was much easier before I structured the theory. My research was going well. I was well-funded and was publishing. I was enjoying developing what I thought were better measures of vagal activity, which I thought provided an easily monitored portal of a protective feature of our nervous system.

For background, the vagus is a cranial nerve that exits the brainstem and travels to the organs in our body. The vagus provides a bidirectional conduit between the brainstem and the visceral organs. Although we generally focus on the motor functions of the vagus and how the motor pathways regulate the heart and the gut, the vagus is primarily a sensory nerve with approximately 80 percent of its fibers sending information from the viscera to the brain. The remaining 20 percent form motor pathways that enable brain circuits to dynamically and, at times, dramatically change our physiology, with some of these changes occurring within seconds. For example, vagal motor pathways can cause our hearts to beat slower and can stimulate our gut.

In its tonic state, the vagus functions like a brake on the

heart's pacemaker. When the brake is removed, the lower vagal tone enables the heart to beat faster. Functionally, the vagal pathways to the heart are inhibitory and slow heart rate. This is often experienced as a calm state. Thus, vagal function is frequently assumed to be an "anti-stress" mechanism.

However, there is other literature contradicting the positive attributes of the vagus and linking vagal mechanisms to life-threatening bradycardia and functionally to sudden death. Basically, the same nerve, the vagus, proposed as an anti-stress system, is capable of stopping the heart and producing defecation in response to life-threatening experiences.

When I studied the autonomic nervous system in graduate school, I was taught that the vagus was the major part of the parasympathetic nervous system, an opposing system to the sympathetic nervous system. Functionally, the sympathetic component of the autonomic nervous system mobilizes the body and gets us moving, while the vagus is involved in calming, growth, and restoration.

In virtually every text on anatomy or physiology, the autonomic nervous system is described as a paired antagonistic system consisting of two opposing components. Metaphorically, we were taught that the sympathetic nervous system, by supporting "stress," was our "mortal enemy," while the parasympathetic nervous system had the capacity to inhibit the debilitating influences of this enemy. The net result was a balance between these antagonistic systems.

In the clinical world, terms like "autonomic balance" are used with an expectation that we should be more parasympathetic and more vagal, so that we are calmer. If we retract this vagal activity and reduce our vagal tone, we become tense and reactive and experience "stress." This concise explanation of the autonomic nervous system story is only partially true. Yes, it is true that most of our visceral organs have neural connections from both the parasympathetic and the sympathetic nervous systems and that most parasympathetic neural fibers travel through the vagus.

For me, the utility of this prevalent model broke down when I was conducting research with human newborns. I was developing new methodologies to measure vagal activity from the beat-to-beat heart rate pattern, which I assumed would index a protective feature that would lead to more positive clinical trajectories. My research was demonstrating that if newborns had a high level of vagal activity (i.e., vagal tone), they had good clinical outcomes. I measured vagal activity by quantifying a rhythmic heart rate pattern known as respiratory sinus arrhythmia. Respiratory sinus arrhythmia is observed as the rhythmic increases and decreases in heart rate associated with spontaneous breathing. However, some babies had beat-to-beat heart rate patterns with a relatively constant beat-to-beat rate and without a respiratory pattern (i.e., no respiratory sinus arrhythmia). These infants were at risk for serious complications.

Based on these findings, I wrote a paper that was published in a journal called *Pediatrics* (Porges, 1992). The goal of the paper was to educate neonatologists and pediatricians about the utility of measuring respiratory sinus arrhythmia, a component of heart rate variability, in the newborn nursery. Following publication of the paper, I received a letter from a neonatologist. The neonatologist wrote that the notion of vagal activity being protective was not consistent with his training. He noted that when he was in medical school, he had learned that the vagus could kill you. I immediately understood what the neonatologist meant. From his perspective, the vagus was capable of promoting life-threatening bradycardia and apnea, characterized by massive slowing of heart rate and cessation of breathing. For many preterm infants, bradycardia and apnea are life-threatening. He then suggested that perhaps too much of a good thing was bad. His comments motivated me to challenge the discontinuities in our understanding of the autonomic nervous system.

I took his comments very seriously and started to think about what I observed in my research. I realized that in my research, I had never observed bradycardia or apnea in the presence of respiratory sinus arrhythmia. With this realization, I framed the vagal paradox. How could the vagus be both protective when it was expressed as respiratory sinus arrhythmia and life-threatening when it was expressed as bradycardia and apnea?

For months, I carried the neonatologist's letter in my briefcase. I tried to explain the paradox. But my knowledge was too limited and I had no explanation. To solve the paradox, I investigated the neuroanatomy of the vagus to find out if there were different vagal circuits regulating these contradictory response patterns.

Identifying the vagal mechanisms underlying the paradox evolved into the Polyvagal Theory. In developing the theory, the anatomy, evolutionary history, and function of two vagal systems were identified: one vagal system mediating bradycardia and apnea and the other vagal system mediating respiratory sinus arrhythmia. One system was potentially lethal, while the other system was potentially protective.

The two vagal pathways originated in different areas of the brainstem. Through the study of comparative anatomy,

I learned that the two circuits evolved sequentially. Basically, we have a built-in hierarchy of autonomic responses based on our phylogenetic history. These facts became the core of the Polyvagal Theory.

Immobilization, bradycardia, and apnea are components of a defense system that evolved in ancient vertebrates long before mammals. We can see this defense system when we observe reptiles in a pet store. When you observe the reptiles, you don't see much behavior, because immobilization is the primary defense system for several reptile species. However, there is a contrast when we watch the behaviors of small mammals, such as hamsters and mice. The small mammals are constantly moving. They are active, they socialize and play with each other, and when they immobilize they are in physical contact with their siblings.

Using evolution as an organizing principle for the Polyvagal Theory, I began to understand that during different phylogenetic stages, different neural circuits were involved in different adaptive behaviors. As I continued my research, I uncovered an ancient defensive system, associated with evolutionarily earlier vertebrates, that is still embedded within our nervous system. This ancient defense system is characterized by immobilization in contrast to the mobilization required for fight and flight defensive behaviors. Although immobilization, feigning death, and appearing to be inanimate are adaptive in many situations for reptiles and other vertebrates, due to mammals' great need for oxygen, it is potentially lethal. If a life-threatening event triggers a biobehavioral response that puts a human into this state of immobilization, it may be very difficult to reorganize to become "normal" again. This is the case for many survivors of trauma.

THE AUTONOMIC NERVOUS SYSTEM REEXPLAINED

As the theory developed, a new model of the adaptive functions of the autonomic nervous system emerged. Within the context of the Polyvagal Theory, the autonomic nervous system states and responses could no longer be explained as the product of the paired antagonism of only parasympathetic and sympathetic components. Rather, explanations of autonomic function need to acknowledge three functional subsystems, which were hierarchically organized as a function of evolutionary biology. In humans and other mammals, these subsystems include: (1) unmyelinated vagal pathways that provide the primary vagal regulation of the organs below the diaphragm; (2) myelinated vagal pathways that provide the primary vagal regulation of the organs above the diaphragm; and (3) the sympathetic nervous system.

The unmyelinated vagal pathways evolved first and are shared with most vertebrates. In humans and other mammals, this ancient system supports homeostasis when the organism is in a safe situation. However, when recruited in defense, it supports immobilization, produces bradycardia and apnea, conserves metabolic resources, and is manifested behaviorally as a shutdown or collapse. In humans, it may also be associated with dissociation. The shutdown system works well for reptiles, because their small brains require much less oxygen than mammals. Reptiles can survive for several hours without breathing. In contrast, even aquatic mammals can hold their breath for only approximately 20 minutes.

The reptilian vagal system represents a phylogenetically ancient vagus that is not myelinated. In contrast to reptiles, mammals have two vagal circuits: an unmyelinated vagus shared with reptiles and a uniquely mammalian circuit that is myelinated. The two vagal circuits originate in different areas of the brainstem. The myelinated pathways provide more rapid and more tightly organized responses. The evolution of the autonomic nervous system in vertebrates starts with the unmyelinated vagus that supports immobilization behaviors. Even cartilaginous fish, such as sharks and rays, have an unmyelinated vagus.

Phylogenetically, starting with bony fish, the sympathetic nervous system comes online and influences visceral organs. The sympathetic nervous system functions as an antagonistic input to the unmyelinated vagus. In most cases, the sympathetic pathways increase and the unmyelinated vagal pathways decrease the activity of visceral organs. An autonomic nervous system characterized by the paired antagonism between the unmyelinated vagus and the sympathetic nervous system enables bony fish to swim in groups, to dart, and to stop.

With mammals, a newer circuit, a uniquely mammalian myelinated vagus, comes online. With the addition of this new vagal circuit, the adaptive functions of the autonomic nervous system expand. First, there is a separation in the roles in which the two vagal pathways regulate bodily organs. The unmyelinated vagus functions as the primary parasympathetic regulator of the organs below the diaphragm. Although in mammals such as premature human newborns, there are sufficient unmyelinated vagal pathways going to the heart to produce bradycardia in the absence of the protective influence of the myelinated vagus. The myelinated vagus functions as the primary parasympathetic regulator of the organs above the diaphragm. In addition, the area in the brainstem from which the new mammalian myelinated vagus originates is linked to the brainstem area that regulates the muscles of the face and head.

Intuitive clinicians know that when they look at their clients' faces and listen to their voices (controlled by muscles of the face and head), they can accurately infer the physiological state of their client. They use this information in determining what they ask of their client. They know that the voice of a traumatized client may lack prosody (intonation in the voice). They know that the upper face of a traumatized client may lack emotional expression. In addition, these same clients frequently have difficulties in regulating their behavioral state and may rapidly transition from a calm to a highly reactive state. Now we can start to see this physiological play acted out in different contexts.

The Polyvagal Theory led to a conceptualization that the autonomic nervous system was not solely a paired antagonistic system, but was a hierarchical system composed of the three subsystems that we have discussed. The hierarchy is organized as a function of evolution, in which newer circuits inhibit older circuits. This hierarchical model is consistent with the construct of dissolution proposed by John Hughlings Jackson (1884) to explain the disinhibition of brain circuits following brain injury and disease.

When we are challenged, the real question is, how and why do we switch into these different circuits? When challenged, the regulation of the autonomic nervous system sequentially degrades to older circuits as an adaptive attempt to survive. What are the cues or the triggers of the process?

We live in a world that has a cognitive bias and assumes that our actions are voluntary. We are confronted with questions related to motivation and outcome. We are asked about costs, risks, and benefits. However, state shifts in the neural regulation of the autonomic nervous system are usually not voluntary, although the state shifts have profound impact on behavior. The state shifts occur in a more reflexive manner when we are confronted by specific cues in the environment. Although clients are frequently unaware of the cues triggering the state change, they are usually aware of their bodily reactions, such as an increase in heart rate, pounding of the heart, and sweating. These responses are involuntary. It is not like they want to do this.

Similar reflexive state shifts are observed in clinical conditions, including aversion to public speaking. If people with this aversion stand up in front of people, they are fearful that they are going to pass out! This is not a voluntary response. Some feature in their environment triggers their nervous system to recruit the unmyelinated vagal circuit.

NEUROCEPTION: DETECTION WITHOUT AWARENESS

Dr. Buczynski: How do our circuits decide which situations are safe?

Dr. Porges: We don't know the exact neural pathways, although the process must involve higher brain structures inhibiting limbic defense systems. We do know that the inhibition of limbic defense circuits may involve cortical areas, including areas of the temporal cortex that evaluate the intentionality of "biological" movement. Biological movement would include facial expressions, intonation of vocalizations (prosody), and body movements, including hand and head gestures. For example, we know the importance of a mother's prosodic voice in calming her infant. However, we know more about the circuits that detect threat than we know about the circuits that detect features of safety.

As more research is conducted, we may learn that early experiences play an important role in changing the threshold or vulnerability for expressing these apparently maladaptive reactions. If we are protected with the newer vagal circuit, we do fine. However, if we lose the capacity of this newer vagal circuit to regulate physiological state, we become a defensive fight/flight machine. When functioning defensively as a fight/flight machine, humans and other mammals need to move. If we are confined, such as being placed in isolation or restrained, our nervous system reads cues and functionally wants to immobilize. I can give you two interesting examples in which these two defense systems were triggered: One is a news clip I saw on CNN, and the second comes from my own experience.

A few years ago, I was at a conference watching a CNN news broadcast before I went to the plenary session to give my talk. The broadcast showed a video clip of an airplane having difficulties as it started to land. The wings were tipping up and down as the airplane was tossed by the wind. Although the airplane looked very unstable, the airplane landed safely. When the passengers disembarked, a reporter interviewed a few passengers. The reporter anticipated that the passengers would say, "I was so scared. I was screaming. I wanted to jump out of my skin." He went up to one of the passengers and asked her to explain how she felt during this unstable landing. Her response left the reporter speechless. She said, "Feel? I passed out."

For this woman, the cues of life threat triggered the ancient vagal circuit. We don't really have control over this circuit. However, losing consciousness has certain advantages that change how we experience a traumatic event, including raising our pain threshold.

Therapists are aware that many people who report abuse, especially sexual abuse and physical abuse that includes restraint, often describe a psychological experience of not really being there. Their bodies may feel numb. They may dissociate or pass out. For these individuals, the abusive event actually triggers an adaptive response that enables them to buffer the sensory and psychological effects of the traumatic event. The problem, of course, is how do you get people back "into their body" once they dissociate and adaptively lose an awareness of their body?

The other example is personal: I experienced an unexpected shift in physiological state when I had an MRI scan. I was quite interested in this procedure, because several of my colleagues conduct research using the MRI. I was curious about the procedure and was looking forward to the experience. To get a brain scan with an MRI, you have to lie down flat on a platform, and the platform is then moved into the core of the magnet. I enthusiastically laid down on the platform and was ready for this new experience. I felt comfortable. I was not anxious. Slowly the platform moved into a very small opening of the MRI magnet. When the top of my head entered the core of the magnet, I said, "Could we wait a moment? Could I get a glass of water?" I was pulled out, and I drank glass of water. I laid down again, and the platform moved until my nose reached the core of the magnet. Then I said, "I can't do this. Get me out!" I couldn't deal with the confined space; it was basically triggering a panic attack.

I use this as an example because my perceptions, my cognitions, were not compatible with my body's response. I wanted to have the MRI. I wasn't scared. It wasn't dangerous. But something happened to my body when I entered the MRI. There were certain cues that my nervous system was detecting, and those cues triggered a defensiveness—wanting me to mobilize, to get out of there.

These experiences of environmental events triggering shifts in physiological state required a new concept to describe the process that evaluates environmental features of risk and triggers the neural circuits to shift autonomic state. This resulted in identifying a process that I labeled "neuroception." I was careful in how I defined the term, because I intended to define a process that was distinct from perception. Perception requires a conscious awareness, while neuroception occurs reflexively without awareness.

Dr. Buczynski: Let's get a definition. Is neuroception the neurological perception of what is going on?

Dr. Porges: Let's be very careful here. We need to distinguish "neuroception" from "perception." Neuroception evaluates risk in the environment without awareness. Perception implies awareness and conscious detection. Neuroception is not a cognitive process; it is a neural process without a dependency on awareness. Neuroception is dependent on a neural circuit that evaluates risk in the environment from a variety of cues and triggers shifts in autonomic state to adaptively deal with the cues. Within Polyvagal Theory, neuroception was postulated as a mechanism to shift the autonomic nervous system into the three broad states defined by the Polyvagal Theory (i.e., safety, danger, life threat) and to emphasize the potent role of the mammalian social engagement system, including the face, heart, and myelinated vagus, in down-regulating both the fight/flight and shutdown defense systems.

When the social engagement system is working, it down-regulates defenses and we feel calm, we hug people, we look at them and we feel good. However, when risk increases, the two defense systems take priority. In response to danger, our sympathetic nervous system takes control and increases metabolic resources to support motor activity for fight/flight behaviors. Then, if that doesn't help us become safe, we recruit the ancient unmyelinated vagal circuit and shut down.

A positive feature of the model that makes it clinically relevant is that it provides insight for developing treatments to down-regulating defense strategies. We know the features of neuroception that trigger the social engagement system, the uniquely mammalian innovation of neural regulation of the autonomic nervous system that enables social interactions to calm physiology and to support health, growth, and restoration.

Dr. Buczynski: Was your experience in the MRI due to neuroception and your response beyond your control?

Dr. Porges: Yes! Similar to the woman who fainted on the airplane, I couldn't do anything about it.

Dr. Buczynski: You couldn't think your way out of it.

Dr. Porges: Not at all! I couldn't even close my eyes and visualize my way out of it. I had to get out of there! Now when I have a MRI, I take medication. I am very appreciative of the fact that drugs can actually enable me not to be reactive in the MRI. Not that I am a big fan of drugs, but under certain conditions they are very helpful.

I want to emphasize that in both of these situations, the woman in the airplane and my MRI, the responses were involuntary. The unstable airplane triggered a shutting down in a passenger, and in my situation, the features of the MRI triggered mobilization. If you were to interview more people on the airplane, some of them may have been screaming and yelling, wanting to mobilize and get out of the airplane. Other passengers may have held the hand of the person next to them and calmly experienced the event.

The critical point here is that the same event can trigger different neuroception reactions in different people, resulting in different physiological states.

Dr. Buczynski: If you had said "Get me out of here" when you were in the MRI machine and no one responded, would you then have reverted to the more primitive?

Dr. Porges: Potentially. Now I am stuck in there and I can't get out. I am in this confined area. What happens to me? This experience is similar to being held down and physically abused. We often forget that medical procedures may convey cues to our body that are similar to physical abuse. We need to be very careful about how people are treated. Even interventions administered with positive intentions that may involve restraint may trigger trauma responses and even PTSD.

TRIGGERING PTSD

Dr. Buczynski: Tell us some of the practices that you think might trigger features of PTSD.

Dr. Porges: I think they include forced physical restraint, even holding a person down for the administration of anesthesia. Looking back into the history of medicine and especially the treatment of the mentally ill, we can see the frequent use of restraint. The justification was to protect the patient, but the patients' responses were more consistent with reacting to injury, danger, or threat. With the mentally ill, restraint was used to keep patients from hurting others or themselves. During surgical procedures when anesthetics were not available or not effective, the patients were restrained.

But remember, several features in the medical environment trigger a sense of vulnerability and a neuroception of defense. For example, medical environments often remove access to the moderating social support features that we have in our normal everyday life. Our clothing is taken away from us. We are put into a public place and predictability is gone. Many of the features that our nervous system uses to self-regulate and to feel safe are not available.

Dr. Buczynski: They tell you not to wear contacts, and then they remove your glasses so you can't see very well.

Dr. Porges: Yes, visual and auditory cues play an important role in determining how neuroception influences our physiological state. One of the most potent triggers of neuroception, or at least the neuroception of safety, is through acoustic stimulation.

If you think about a mother singing a lullaby to her baby or about listening to traditional folk music or love songs, there is a similarity in the acoustic features of these different types of vocal music. These examples do not use low-frequency sounds, and the higher frequencies that you are hearing are actively being modulated. The sounds are similar to a female voice. A lullaby will not have the same calming effect on the infant if sung with the low frequencies of a male voice, especially in the range of a bass. Our nervous system responds to both the frequency band and the modulation of acoustic frequencies within the frequency band.

In my talks, I use *Peter and the Wolf* as an example of how frequency band and modulation of the frequencies within a band can trigger neuroception. In *Peter and the Wolf*, the friendly characters are represented by the music produced by violins, clarinet, flute, and oboe. The predator is conveyed via lower-frequency sounds. Prokofiev had an intuitive understanding of the effectiveness of acoustic stimulation in the process of neuroception and used this intuition in framing the narrative.

What are the acoustic features of the MRI? The MRI produces massive amounts of low-frequency sounds. In general, the acoustic features of hospitals are dominated by low-frequency noises, especially sounds produced by ventilation systems and equipment. Our nervous system responds, without our awareness, to these acoustic features and interprets acoustic stimulation as a feature of a predator and shifts our physiological state to promote either fight/flight behaviors or shutdown.

THE ROLE OF SOCIAL ENGAGEMENT AND ATTACHMENT

Dr. Buczynski: Let's talk a little bit about attachment. How does early attachment affect all this?

Dr. Porges: In surveying the literature on attachment, I noticed that an important point seems to be missing. I call the missing point the preamble to attachment. In Polyvagal Theory, this missing point is described as social engagement. In my conceptualization, I started partitioning the development of a good social bond as two sequential processes: social engagement and the establishment of social bonds.

Let's start with social engagement. This is the process in which we use vocalization, we use listening to intonation in the voice, we use facial expressions, and we use gestures. We also use ingestive behaviors such as a baby nursing. When we are adults, we use the same systems in different contexts. We go out to lunch or we go out for a drink as a way of socializing. Ingestive behaviors use the same neural mechanisms that we use for social behavior. In a sense, we use ingestive behaviors to calm people down and to socially engage others. When social engagement is effective, psychological distance between people is minimized, which leads to a reduction in physical distance.

As we observe development, we notice that young infants are less discriminatory early in life regarding with whom they socially interact. There is tremendous plasticity in the system for babies to be held by many different people. But as the baby gets older, the process of neuroception, which detects features of safety, becomes more and more selective in identifying familiarity and defining safety before the baby can be held.

I work with autistic children, and one of the features that the parents report is that the child is afraid of their father. What do they mean by that? They mean that the child is afraid of the father's voice. Why? Because the voice is characterized by low frequency sounds, which through evolution are wired to neural circuits that adaptively detect predator. Thus, we understand that many of the behaviors we observe in clinical disorders are actually adaptive behaviors that are triggered by neuroception often misinterpreting the intention of the cues.

Let's return to your question about attachment. I think that safety moderates the ability to develop secure attachments. Whether or not an individual feels safe with the parent, caregiver, family members, or others during early development might moderate individual differences in vulnerability to trauma.

WHAT DO AUTISM AND TRAUMA HAVE IN COMMON?

Dr. Buczynski: You raised the issues of autism and trauma just now. When I was preparing for our call, I was thinking that there are a lot of similarities between autism and trauma in terms of what is going on auditorily.

Dr. Porges: Yes, I think there is a common core of features among several psychiatric diagnostic categories. Not a common cause, but more like a shared effect. However, the views of science and clinical practice often approach features of disease and health differently. Science is interested in processes, while clinical practice is often interested in a disease entity or specificity of diagnosis. There has long been an assumption that if you can give the disorder a name, it will lead to improved treatment and will provide a better understanding of the disorder. However, it appears that diagnoses, especially within the area of mental health, have had a greater impact on the finances of clinicians than on understanding the mechanisms underlying the disorder that would lead to improved treatment. In general, diagnostic labels provide the clinician with the ability to use certain billing codes required by insurance, although labeling psychiatric disorders have had little impact on understanding underlying neurophysiological mechanisms.

Scientists are less interested in the labels associated with clinical diagnoses and more interested in the underlying processes. There are several underlying processes that cross several clinical disorders. These common processes frequently are not of interest to federal funding agencies and disease-specific foundations. Research focusing on these common processes is limited and frequently goes unfunded, since funding sources are directed toward identifying "biomarkers" assumed to be specific to a clinical diagnosis. Unfortunately, although virtually every mental health disorder is assumed to be biological and is often considered to involve genetics or brain structures, decades of research searching for an elusive biomarker or biological signature has been far from impressive.

One common process that is observed in several mental health diagnoses is auditory hypersensitivities. Since auditory hypersensitivity is not specific to any clinical disorder and is not a specific criterion contributing to a diagnosis, it has not stimulated much interest within the mental health research community. However, by understanding the underlying mechanisms that contribute to auditory hypersensitivities, we learn that there is a neural circuit that relates auditory hypersensitivities to flat facial affect, poor vocal prosody, and dampened vagal control of the heart.

When individuals with a trauma history are carefully observed and interviewed, we immediately learn that they don't like to be in public places because noise or sounds bother them, and they frequently have great difficulty extracting human voice from background activity. Many individuals with autism report the same problems. Autistic individuals frequently suffer from a hearing/listening paradox in which they are hypersensitive to sound but have great difficulty in extracting and understanding human voice.

If we observe individuals with other psychiatric disorders, such as depression and schizophrenia, we see similar features. Not only do individuals with these disorders have auditory hypersensitivities, but they have behavioral state regulation difficulties, a flatness of affective tone expressed on their faces, a lack of prosody in their voices, and an autonomic state characterized by higher heart rates and less vagal regulation of their heart that would support defensive behaviors. These core processes related to the expression and detection of emotion are integrated into a "social engagement system" that is regulated in a part of the brainstem that regulates the mammalian or new vagal system.

A person who has an expressive face and a prosodic voice is also contracting middle ear muscles that facilitate the extraction of human voice from background sounds. When people are smiling and looking at the person speaking, their middle ear muscles are contracting. In this state, they are better able to extract human voice from background sounds, but they are doing this at a price.

The "adaptive" price we, as humans, pay for social behavior is the critical point that explains how Polyvagal Theory informs our understanding of psychiatric disorders. We pay a price by down-regulating our ability to hear low-frequency sounds, sounds that through our phylogenetic history were associated with predator. For individuals with autism, PTSD, and various other clinical disorders, the social engagement system and the ability to down-regulate defensive systems are compromised. However, a compromised social engagement system functionally provides an advantage in detecting predator. A down-regulated social engagement system enables individuals to know if someone is walking behind them. In this biobehavioral state, they can hear low-frequency background sounds but now have difficulties in extracting meaning from the higher frequencies associated with human voices.

Dr. Buczynski: Is that because something is different in their middle ear structures?

Dr. Porges: Well, in part. But we do not assume that these differences are permanent. Here is an example. What town do you live in?

Dr. Buczynski: I live in Storrs, Connecticut.

Dr. Porges: Okay. If you were to walk through New Haven when it wasn't very safe, and you were walking with someone else and that person was talking to you, would you understand what that person was saying? Or would you hear the footsteps behind you?

Dr. Buczynski: I'd be in a careful mode.

Dr. Porges: The careful mode is that you wouldn't really hear what the person is saying, but you would hear the steps behind you. When we enter new environments, which are potentially dangerous, we shift to a surveillance vigilance system from a safe social engagement system. From a cognitive perspective, we use terms like allocation of attention. But from a neurophysiological model, it is not simply allocation of attention. We have shifted physiological state. We have reduced the neural tone to the middle ear structures so that we are better able to hear low-frequency predator sounds. But if we do that, there is an expense; we now have difficulties in hearing and understanding human voice.

Dr. Buczynski: And I did that involuntarily?

Dr. Porges: Yes! One hopes! Because if you are focusing on human voice, you might miss things that might be a real threat to your life.

Dr. Buczynski: Let's say that people aren't picking up on danger when they should be. What is structurally, physiologically, going on?

Dr. Porges: If they are not picking up on danger and they remain focused on human voice, their nervous system has prioritized the social features of vocalizations over the danger features of a potential predator.

You can see variations among people in how the nervous system prioritizes safety and risk factors. If you are part of a group that enters a novel environment, some people reflexively become hypervigilant and stop participating in the group discussions, while others keep socially talking to each other until someone comes up behind them and something dangerous happens.

If we use a model that emphasizes the adaptiveness of the neural regulation of middle ear structures, we can ask questions about the potential role of neural regulation of the middle ear muscles in language delays in various subpopulations. If a child comes from a dangerous neighborhood or an unsafe family, will the child have language delays? Children who live in these environments are usually tuned to pick up predator, and their nervous system will not easily give up the ability to detect predator. Will their language delay be due to their inability to clearly hear human voice? When the middle ear muscles are not appropriately tuned to extract human voice, the individual has difficulties extracting the meaning of words. When the tone of the middle ear muscles is weak, the higher-frequency harmonics associated with consonants are muffled. The individual may know that someone is speaking but does not understand what the sounds mean.

Dr. Buczynski: They can hear chatter, but they can't absorb the meaning of it?

Dr. Porges: Yes. Because the features of human voice that convey meaning rely on the detection of the consonants at the ends of words, which are characterized by frequencies higher than the fundamental frequency of the vowels. I'll give you another example. A natural function of aging is the loss of ability to accurately hear high frequencies, and this compromises our ability to understand what people are saying, especially when there is background noise.

Dr. Buczynski: Some of us, yes!

Dr. Porges: Some of us, but not all of us! As mature adults, when we enter a bar or noisy restaurant and people talk to us, do we hear the ends of their words? We know they are speaking, we can hear sounds, but can we understand what they are saying? However, when we think back to when we were teenagers or in college, we remember that when we went to concerts and bars, we were able to meet new people, to listen, and to talk in environments that we would now perceive as noisy.

When we were younger, words were never lost; we heard everything. We could understand what people were saying because we had a functional neural system that effectively regulated the middle ear structures, and this changed as we matured. But what would our language and social skills be if we started out that way? If our middle ear neural regulation was compromised the way it is in older people and we had to learn a language like a young infant, we might have had great difficulty. We would have had difficulty extracting the words from the background noise. I think this is the sensory world that is experienced by many children with autism.

TREATMENT OF AUTISM DISORDERS

Dr. Buczynski: I want to switch us into what this means to treatment. Since we are talking about autistic children, let's start there, and then we will circle back and focus on treating people with PTSD.

Dr. Porges: We can cluster both PTSD and autism together, because from a Polyvagal perspective, the pivotal point is whether we can help another human feel safe. Safety is a powerful construct that involves features from several processes and domains, including context, behavior, mental processes, and physiological state. If we feel safe, we have access to the neural regulation of the facial muscles. We have access to a myelinated vagal circuit that is capable of down-regulating the commonly observed fight/flight and stress responses. And, when we down-regulate our defense, we have an opportunity to play and to enjoy our social interactions.

I wanted to introduce into this discussion the concept of play. An inability to play is a characteristic of many individuals with a psychiatric diagnosis. Yet, we do not find an inability to play with others or to spontaneously and reciprocally express humor in any diagnostic criteria.

I do not consider solitary activities such as "playing" with video games, computers, or toys as play. Instead, my perspective of play requires social interaction. Play requires an ability to mobilize with the sympathetic nervous system and then to down-regulate the sympathetic excitation with face-to-face social interaction and the social engagement system. Within this model, play is an efficient neural exercise using social interactions to "co-regulate" physiological and behavioral state. In contrast, solitary interactions with objects such as computers and video games are attempts to self-regulate.

Dr. Buczynski: Say that again—I want to make sure everyone has that. What does play require?

Dr. Porges: As an example, I will describe how my dogs play. I have two little dogs, Japanese Chins, and they weigh about 8 pounds each. They frequently chase each other as they run through the house. In this game of chase, one dog tries to catch the other by biting the other dog's rear leg. When this happens, the one that has been bitten will turn around to look at the other. This face-to-face interaction is critical in distinguishing play from aggressive behaviors. The face-to-face interaction provides the cues to assure the dog that was being bitten that the biting behavior was play and not aggression. In this case, the social engagement system, through the use of face-to-face interactions, functionally contains and down-regulates the mobilization behavior to ensure that it is not amplified and transformed into aggressive fight/flight behavior.

In my talks, I show video clips of two famous and now long retired basketball players, Dr. J and Larry Bird. I start off with a clip in which they appear to be good friends. They are doing an advertisement for basketball shoes. Then I show a clip of them playing basketball against each other in which there is a lot of physical contact. They are bumping and hitting each other. During this active physical contact, Dr. J appears to accidently hit Larry Bird in the face. Bird falls to the ground and Dr. J walks away without looking at Bird. By walking away, Dr. J doesn't provide the necessary cues to Bird that would distinguish his mobilization behaviors as play rather than fight/flight. Bird's body reacts defensively and goes after Dr. J, pushes him, and they start throwing punches at each other.

These examples provide us with an understanding of how people and other mammals use face-to-face interactions to repair a violation of expectancy. When we play, we mobilize with physiological state changes that are capable of supporting fight/flight defensive behaviors. Then we down-regulate defensive reactions by looking at each other. If we hit each other by mistake, we say, "I'm sorry." We use our voice and facial expression to reduce the possibility that the behavior will be interpreted by the nervous system as aggressive.

Play often requires mobilization. But, to make sure mobilization isn't transformed into aggressiveness, play requires face-to-face interactions. During play, we start seeing a behavioral reciprocity that involves movements similar to fight/flight behaviors that are followed by face-to-face interactions. We see this in the play of virtually all mammals.

We can describe other expressions of adult play with similar reciprocal features of movement and inhibition of movement aided by face-to-face interactions, such as dancing. Most forms of team sports involve face-to-face interactions that include communication via eye contact, and when face-to-face interactions are not a viable option, vocal communication is used.

Exercising on a treadmill is not play. Play from a polyvagal perspective is not solitary; it is interactive and requires face-to-face interactions and the use of other features of the social engagement system, including prosodic voice.

Within this perspective, play is not practice for aggressiveness. Rather, play is functionally a neural exercise of using the social engagement system, a uniquely mammalian system, to down-regulate our fight/flight behaviors, to be able to contain and "socialize" this defensive system. Play is a neural exercise in which we regulate a phylogenetically older system (mobilization based on excitation of the sympathetic nervous system) with a newer system (social engagement with myelinated vagal pathways). However, it is important to note that individuals with several clinical pathologies often have difficulty playing.

Dr. Buczynski: Let's tie that to treatment.

Dr. Porges: The issue with treatment is that feeling safe is functionally the prerequisite state that enables successful treatment to occur. Many successful treatments function as neural exercises recruiting this safe state to provide the client with a personal resource to down-regulate defensive strategies to promote state regulation through the social engagement system. Recruitment of the social engagement system through face-to-face interactions functions as a neural exercise recruiting myelinated vagal pathways to dampen sympathetic activity. Play literally becomes a functional therapeutic model that exercises the neural regulation of autonomic state through reciprocal social interactions. Even traditional talk therapy can be conceptualized as a neural exercise.

A relatively efficient method to enhance feelings of safety in clients is to change the physical features of the clinical environment. Clinicians can remove sounds that reflexively, through neuroception, would have triggered defensive states and provide sounds that calm and signal safety. Removing low-frequency sounds that our nervous system detects as predator is helpful. The addition of soft vocal music or prosodic vocalization may be calming to the client. Clinicians need to engage their clients with a prosodic voice characterized by variations in intonation. They need to use modulations in intonation and not modulations in loudness to calm and reassure their clients and to move their clients into a state of safety. If they rely on modulations in loudness, the client's nervous system may feel that they are being attacked and reflexively shift into a physiological state that supports defense. Since physiological state contributes to clients' reactions and feelings, clinicians need to respect the powerful role of neuroception and capitalize on understanding how to use contextual cues in the clinical setting to move the client into a calmer, more trusting state. As the therapist is informed about the client's neuroceptive sensitivity to becoming defensive, the therapist gains insights into how to manage the client and how to build resilience through neural exercises involving the social engagement system. During these neural exercises, both the therapist and the client gain a better understanding of the "reflexive" triggers of defense. This process provides the client with an understanding of the important role of physiological state in both prosocial behaviors and in response to trauma. This understanding reduces the shame associated with assuming that the disorder is related to a voluntary decision, a stigma that clients experience.

I am not talking about curing; I am talking about reducing some of the symptoms to make life better for people with disorders. If we understand that physiological state provides a functional platform for different classes of behavior, then we are aware that when a client is in a physiological state that supports fight/flight, the client will not be available for social behavior. If the client is in a physiological state of shutting down, the client is functionally immune to social interactions. An important treatment goal is to provide the client with the ability to access the physiological state that enables social engagement. In developing this capacity, the client is informed that access to this physiological state is limited, due to our neuroception processes, to safe environments. With that knowledge, we need to structure settings to remove sensory cues that trigger a neuroception of danger and life threat. The removal of low-frequency sounds would be a good start.

Dr. Buczynski: Would hospitals need to sound-insulate their rooms?

Dr. Porges: Yes, they would need to create "safe zones" that trigger through neuroception a physiological state of safety. Hospitals need these safe zones, not zones of vulnerability. If you are admitted as a patient in a hospital, there are few places where you could feel "safe." Your personal space is going to be invaded. Many of us have had that experience.

Dr. Buczynski: Yes. But what does that mean?

Dr. Porges: It means that you are not safe in hospitals. It means that your body is in a state that will support defense and not health and restoration. Being in a defensive state interferes with recovery. Psychologically, you will replace trust with hypervigilance. And that means that your social engagement system is going to be turned off, because the social engagement system is not accessible in environments in which people are poking things at you.

Dr. Buczynski: Yes. They might give you the schedule so that you would have some sense of predictability.

Dr. Porges: Our nervous system likes predictability.

Dr. Buczynski: How about with trauma, PTSD patients?

Dr. Porges: In my talks, I started to tell clinicians, "Try something different with clients." I said, "Tell your clients, who were traumatized, that they should celebrate their body's responses, even if the profound physiological and behavioral states that they have experienced currently limit their ability to function in a social world. They should celebrate their body's responses, since these responses enabled them to survive. It saved their lives. It reduced some of the injury. If they were oppositional during an aggressive traumatic event, such as rape, they could have been killed. Tell them to celebrate how their body responded instead of making them feel guilty that their body failed them when they wanted to be social, and let's see what happens."

When clinicians told their clients this simple message, I started to receive emails about how their clients improved spontaneously. I think this occurred because the clients started to see themselves as not having done something bad.

This is consistent with another point I frequently make, which is that there is no such thing as a bad response. There are only adaptive responses. The primary point is that our nervous system is trying to do the right thing for us to survive, and we need to respect what it has done. When we respect our body's responses, we move from this more evaluative state, we become more respectful of ourselves, and this functionally contributes to the healing process.

Now, remember, what is occurring in most therapies? Therapies often convey to the client that their body is not behaving adequately. The clients are told they need to be different. They need to change. So therapy in itself is extraordinarily evaluative of the individual. And once we are evaluated, we are basically in defensive states. We are not in safe states.

Dr. Buczynski: And teaching is, as well.

Dr. Porges: Yes. I have given a few lectures on mindfulness, and in these lectures I state that mindfulness requires feeling safe. Because, if we don't feel safe, we are neurophysiologically evaluative of our setting, which precludes feeling safe. In this defensive state, we can't engage others and we can't recruit the wonderful neural circuits that enable us to express the expansive, creative, and benevolent aspects of being human. If we are able to create safe environments, we have access to neural circuits that enable us to be social, to learn, and to feel good.

THE LISTENING PROJECT PROTOCOL: THEORY AND TREATMENT

Dr. Buczynski: You have an intervention project that I think people would like to know about.

Dr. Porges: Yes. I have been conducting research on this intervention since the late 1990s, when I tried out a technology to stimulate features of the Polyvagal Theory. The Polyvagal Theory, especially the part of the theory that emphasizes the social engagement system, assumes that if we use prosodic vocalizations to engage the middle ear muscles, the muscles that help us extract human voice from background sound, via neural feedback, this form of active listening will change physiological state and enable the individual to be more spontaneously social. This system is observed when a mother uses an extremely modulated voice to calm her infant and should be triggered when we listen to voices that are very prosodic with great variation in pitch. It is a parsimonious model that focuses on providing the nervous system with acoustic cues that trigger a neuroception of safety. When we started testing the intervention with children with autism, we got amazing effects (see Porges et. al., 2013; Porges et. al. 2014).

During the past decade, more than 200 children and several adults have participated in our research applying the listening intervention. We observed reductions in auditory hypersensitivities, improved auditory processing, increases in spontaneous social behavior, and increased vagal regulation of the heart (i.e., respiratory sinus arrhythmia).

Dr. Buczynski: Those 200 people—were they autistic?

Dr. Porges: Yes, most carried the full diagnosis. However, your question triggers additional questions about conducting research with autistic individuals. After I started working with autistic children, I realized that autism, as a diagnostic category, was not a very specific diagnosis and that there were variations in symptoms and function. I decided that if I focused on auditory hypersensitivities, I could move into an area that would be helpful and wouldn't be viewed as controversial, such as trying to cure autism—especially since the defining diagnostic features of autism didn't seem to be well organized or fit a common neurophysiological basis.

Autism is a very complicated disorder that involves not only the individual with the diagnosis, but also impacts the family. When there is talk of curing autism, it sparks controversy in the research community. Since the diagnosis assumes a lifelong disorder based on an unidentified genetic cause and an unidentified manifestation in brain/nervous system function, the psychiatric community interprets a reversal of symptoms as being due to a faulty diagnosis and not a true recovery. To stay clear of the controversy, I directed my intervention research strategy toward auditory hypersensitivities.

To objectify the mechanisms through which the intervention worked, my research team needed to develop an objective measure of the function of the middle ear structures. During the past decade, I developed with my former graduate student, Greg Lewis, a device to measure the middle ear transfer function and to identify what sounds actually get through the middle ear on their journey to the brain. We called this device the middle ear sound absorption system, or MESAS (Porges & Lewis, 2011). With MESAS, we are able to measure whether or not the Listening Project Protocol changes the acoustic features of sounds that actually get into the brain or bounce off of the eardrum. We have piloted with MESAS and are now using MESAS in three clinical trials evaluating the Listening Project Protocol. When the middle ear muscles tense, the higher frequencies of human voice pass through the middle ear structures and go through the auditory nerve to the brain, and much of the acoustic energy of lower frequency sounds bounces off the eardrum. The eardrum is very much like a kettledrum. If the middle ear muscles functionally tighten the eardrum, the softer, higher-pitch sounds get through to the brain. If the middle ear muscles lose their tone, the eardrum is more pliable and the louder, lower-pitch sounds get through to the brain and the higher-pitch sounds are lost in background noise.

When we hear lower-pitch sounds, our nervous system maintains a bias toward the detection of low-pitch sounds as preparation to detect movements of a predator. With this advantage to hear predator comes difficulties hearing human voice. MESAS provides an ability to objectively measure the functional impact of the middle ear muscles on auditory processing.

MESAS can be used to quantify individual differences in the middle ear transfer function and to identify vulnerabilities related to difficulties in understanding voice in background noise. Even within the restrictive range of normal people, we can see the effect. The device can now objectively measure changes in function in response to the treatment. This is a big breakthrough, because prior to the development of this device, the ability to evaluate auditory hypersensitivities was solely subjective. When you deal with children who have language problems, you need to ask their parents for information about the child's subjective experiences, and the parents have to be accurate observers of their child to provide valid information.

After participating in the Listening Project Protocol, a father related an interesting story about his autistic son. Prior to the intervention, he would put his fingers in his ears when sounds bothered him. Placing fingers in the ears is a common response to noise for autistic children. This past year, the son participated in the Special Olympics. His father told me that when the starting pistol was shot, all the other kids on the starting line stopped and put their fingers in their ears, but he didn't. He just ran and won.

The point is that auditory hypersensitivities are now treatable in many of the children with the method we developed. But another very important feature usually accompanies the reduction of auditory hypersensitivity: improved auditory processing. With the reduced auditory hypersensitivities, the individual is better able to process human voice and there are improvements in language development. Although I have not tried this with PTSD, we are currently testing the intervention with children with abuse histories. The preliminary findings are positive.

Dr. Buczynski: I understand that you have a way to measure this with the child. But then, once you have a sense that this is happening, what did you do with this child to treat him?

Dr. Porges: I didn't explain the listening project—thank you for putting me back on track! The Listening Project Protocol is really quite simple. It is listening to acoustic stimulation. In the Listening Project Protocol, we use vocal music, because we want to emphasize the prosodic features of the human voice. Remember what I was saying about prosodic features. If we listen to a voice characterized by a great degree of tonal modulation, our nervous system functionally starts triggering a state associated with safety.

With this knowledge, we amplified the prosodic features of the vocal music by custom-designed computer algorithms that processed the music. If you were to listen to it, it would sound at times like the music was disappearing. It would sound very thin, and then it would become richer, and then thinner again. As the sounds disappeared, you might try harder to hear it, and you might feel a subjective feeling of loss. When the sound started to return, you might feel a sense of exuberance.

By modulating the frequency bands, we subjectively feel pulled in and out of the acoustic environment. The objective of the intervention was to trigger the neural circuits involved with a neuroception of safety, which are normally triggered by prosodic voices similar to a mother calming her infant. The intervention amplifies prosody and not volume. This means that the intervention makes the acoustic features of the vocalizations more melodic, with more variations in intonation. In addition, the low-frequency sounds that would normally trigger defenses are removed. These modified acoustic stimuli are delivered to the child in a quiet room, which respects the fact that the child might have difficulty in dealing with other forms of stimulation, including interactions with other humans.

The intervention is driven by two features: first, to keep the child in a calm physiological state that supports feelings of safety, and second, to expose the child to the modulated acoustic stimulation. Only when the nervous system is not required to be hypervigilant and defensive can it regulate the middle ear muscles to allow the child to experience the neurophysiological benefits of the modulated sounds.

From my perspective, the intervention is a neural exercise requiring passive listening to sounds that trigger the nervous system's need for or prewired interest in prosodic vocalizations. Observing children participating in the intervention provides an opportunity to see the neural circuit regulating the entire social engagement system come online. In many of the children, the facial muscles become more animated. Prosody is increased in children's vocalizations, as the children are better able to listen to their own voices. Functionally, the intervention also enhances vagal regulation of the heart, which calms physiological state and makes voices more prosodic. [The Listening Project Protocol is now available to clinicians through Integrated Listening Systems as the Safe and Sound Protocol: A Portal to Social Engagement. http://integratedilstening.com/ssp-safe-sound-protocol/].

HOW MUSIC SUPPORTS INTIMACY: CUES OF SAFETY

Dr. Porges: Do you remember the singer Johnny Mathis?

Dr. Buczynski: Oh, yes!

Dr. Porges: You said that with kind of a wistful intonation. Please tell me what you remember of Johnny Mathis's voice.

Dr. Buczynski: Oh, it was sweet and melodic.

Dr. Porges: Yes, and physiologically, when it was played, how did you feel?

Dr. Buczynski: Calm and like singing along.

Dr. Porges: Was it ever used in certain social settings when you were growing up?

Dr. Buczynski: It might have been!

Dr. Porges: It was basically used when adolescents were trying to get physically closer to each other, correct?

Dr. Buczynski: Exactly!

Dr. Porges: What we didn't know at that time was that the prosodic features of Johnny Mathis's voice were triggering the neuroception circuit that would make us feel safe. And when we felt safe, we could enjoy physical contact. In a sense, defensiveness was greatly diffused by Johnny Mathis. If you think about your bodily and subjective responses to listening to Johnny Mathis, you will have an intuitive understanding of how the listening therapy works. Modulating the frequency bands in the vocal range in which Johnny Mathis sings, similar to a mother singing a lullaby to her baby, triggers a neural circuit that enables a human being to feel safer. Even when you visualized and thought about Johnny Mathis singing, your voice started to have different intonation as well.

The Listening Project Protocol is not a long-term intensive intervention. It is only five one-hour sessions. The effects, if they are going to occur, normally start to be observed after the third day. The first two days are really for the child to get used to the intervention environment.

I want to emphasize that our nervous system is metaphorically waiting for Johnny Mathis to turn off our defenses. We are sitting there waiting for intonation of voice. When we detect prosodic voices, the neural response to these sounds changes our physiological state.

In contrast to the seductive impact of a prosodic voice, the caricature of a boring college professor includes speaking in a monotone, which provides another example of how neuroception shifts physiological state. However, the monotonous voice leads to loss of interest and sleepiness. Many might recall the role that Ben Stein frequently played, which was a caricature of this persona. When a person talks in a monotone, it is difficult to understand what they are saying. The listener is not pulled into the discussion, because the voice is not seductively engaging us to extract the information. An understanding of how the voice attracts interest and attention is minimized in our cognitive world, especially within the educational system.

Our cognitive world focuses on the content of the words, not on the intonation upon which the words are being conveyed.

Therapists need to understand that the cues of a therapeutic setting are extremely critical to the success of the therapeutic process. Background sounds can change the physiological state of clients and limit the client's accessibility to therapy. In addition, it is not just the words clinicians use in their therapy sessions; it also how they use vocal intonations to trigger a neuroception of safety in their clients. Insight may do far less in therapy than the acoustic properties of the therapeutic setting and the therapist's vocal intonations.

Dr. Buczynski: This training of the middle ear muscles that you do with autistic children—have you ever tried doing that with an aging population to see if you could help them recover some of their ability to separate background sounds so that they can hear better?

Dr. Porges: I have thought of doing this. Your intuitions are correct. Aging also contributes to a functional deterioration of the system. I decided to experience the effects of the intervention stimuli and to determine if there were any effects of prolonging the intervention. I wanted to find out what happened if I overdosed! Initially, my concern was related to fatigue, since the intervention was targeted at stimulating very small fast twitch muscles that may rapidly fatigue.

I listened to the acoustic stimulation from the Listening Project Protocol for six to eight hours a day for a few days. I became so sensitive to higher frequencies that I couldn't even sit at my desk with my computer running, because now the computer fan was too loud. I could hear the high-frequency sounds, sounds that normally dissipate within a short distance. I could hear my children talking even when they were in rooms at the other end of our house. I got so tuned to the frequency band of human voices that I couldn't ignore it. It took two weeks to return to a normal hearing sensitivity. Now I am more cautious and very respectful of individual sensitivities and vulnerabilities.

As I formulated the parameters for the Listening Project Protocol, I was informed by knowledge of the neural regulation of the very small middle ear muscles, which rapidly fatigue. When the muscles fatigue, the body detects exhaustion. Feelings of exhaustion have been reported by several participants during the Listening Project Protocol even though they were listening for only an hour each day. We have received reports that participants often sleep well following the intervention sessions. I have speculated that the exhaustion was due to these very small muscles fatiguing and sending feedback to the nervous system of this fatigue. It appears that the feedback from these small muscles may provide as powerful a feedback signal as the fatigue experienced to larger muscles after running a few miles.

Dr. Buczynski: If they use those muscles more and more, will they build up endurance?

Dr. Porges: Yes. For many individuals with normal listening and social engagement behaviors, the tone of the middle ear muscles is greater. However, for many, the neural tone has retracted to promote states that provide lower thresholds to predator sounds. This retraction may have occurred in response to illness and fever or in response to traumatic events (i.e., exposure to danger and life threat cues). Once the circuit is triggered in the appropriately safe environment, the positive attributes of social engagement provide a social reward and the system continues to be used. In a sense, the contraction of the middle ear muscles will be mutually rewarding in the social setting. When a child talks to his or her parents and the parents look back to the child, the family unit defines an interactive feedback loop, and the child will talk and listen more.

However, not all parents reciprocally engage their child when their child engages them. I often have children of professionals coming to my laboratory for the intervention. At a conference when I saw a parent of a child who had participated in the intervention research, I asked him how his son was doing. In response to my question, the father broke eye contact, turned 90 degrees from me, and said, "He's doing very well." The father's behavior violated the expectancy of my social engagement system. I said to the father, "If you turn away when you talk to him, he's going to have problems quickly again. You can't turn away from your son. Even if you do this involuntarily, you are going to have to self-monitor." If the father keeps turning away, it will turn off the child's social engagement system.

As a species, we are very adaptive. If we come from families where parents are depressed or chaotic, we will adapt by not engaging them, and we literally will down-regulate our social engagement system. But as we down-regulate the social engagement system, we start picking up symptoms of other clinical disorders. It doesn't mean that we are locked into those disorders for life. It means that the system is down-regulated, but may be available if prompted with the appropriate stimuli. The Listening Project Protocol was developed to awaken a dormant social engagement system and to optimize the function of the social engagement system, even if the system appears to be compromised.

Dr. Buczynski: Stephen, thank you for your work. It is life changing, I am sure, for many, many people. This is a paradigm shift, and I just want to say thank you and I have so much respect for what you have done.

3

SELF-REGULATION AND SOCIAL ENGAGEMENT

Stephen W. Porges and Ruth Buczynski

HEART RATE VARIABILITY AND SELF-REGULATION: WHAT'S THE RELATIONSHIP?

Dr. Buczynski: We hear how our unconscious functions—heart rate, respiration—are vaguely related to social relationships such as trust and intimacy. If they are, they would have a huge impact on treatment—our treatment of anxiety, depression, trauma, and even our treatment of autism.

But it's not just that the nervous system influences our interaction with others. The reverse is also true; our interactions with others influence the nervous system. Stephen, you've observed that people who have some stability in their heart rate and people who are more able to self-regulate seem to be different, in terms of how they respond to trauma and other experiences, than people who don't have stability in their heart rate and can't self-regulate it.

Dr. Porges: The ability to observe heart rate patterns is literally a portal to watch how our nervous system is regulating our bodies. When the pattern of heart rate is showing nice periodic oscillations, it's basically telling us that we're in a good state; it's reflecting a homeostatic system that is regulating well.

When this system is challenged, the neural feedback—from the periphery, from our viscera, from our heart—to our brain, changes, and is reflected in the vagal regulation of the heart. The vagal regulation of the heart is dynamically reflected in the amplitude of a periodic component embedded in heart rate variability known as respiratory sinus arrhythmia.

Rather than talking about physiological correlates of psychological experiences, think of physiological responses more as a dynamic window of the nervous system's ability to adjust to various challenges and how our body is reflecting those adjustments.

THE ORGANIZING PRINCIPLES OF POLYVAGAL THEORY

Dr. Buczynski: Your theory provides the organizing principles behind the observation, and I would say that you are tying together some pretty disparate fields, scientific fields and treatment fields. What are your thoughts on that?

Dr. Porges: This has been a lifelong journey to basically understand how our physiology was related to our mental and behavioral states. It has been a wonderful experience, since I have been able to use my research and profession to explore ideas about how our nervous system functions—really how we function in a complex environment.

The concepts underlying the Polyvagal Theory are relatively basic, but they were elusive. They were elusive for decades if not centuries. They were uncovered by a shift in orientation and an attempt to understand nervous system responses to challenges from an evolutionary perspective and to see shifts in physiology and behavior as adaptive strategies linked to survival. For mammals, the adaptive strategies functionally are a recapitulation of our phylogenetic history. It follows how the neural regulation of the autonomic nervous system shifted during vertebrate evolution, especially as mammals emerged from ancient extinct reptiles.

Dr. Buczynski: This evolution is not just the biological evolution, but the genetic evolution.

Dr. Porges: Yes. The systems changed and provided mammals, which we are, with various adaptive functions. So the real issue in understanding the Polyvagal Theory is to realize that humans, being mammals, need other mammals, other humans, to interact with to survive.

The important aspect is really the ability to reciprocally interact, to reciprocally regulate each other's physiological state, and basically create relationships to enable individuals to feel safe.

If we see this as a theme through all aspects of human development and even aging, then concepts like attachment start to make sense, as do concepts like intimacy, love, and friendship. But then again, concepts like bullying and having problems with individuals or spousal conflict also start to make sense. Oppositional behavior in the classroom starts making sense. Basically, our nervous system craves reciprocal interaction to enable state regulation to feel safe. And disruptions to this ability to have reciprocal interactions become a feature of dysfunctional development.

Now, that being said, people have thought that's behavioral, not physiological. But the Polyvagal Theory informs us that it is physiological, and that the neural pathways of social support and social behavior are shared with the neural pathways that support health, growth, and restoration. They are the same pathways. Mind–body and brain–body sciences are not correlative; they're the same thing from different perspectives.

Dr. Buczynski: I want to get you to repeat that: The neural pathways are shared.

Dr. Porges: There are neural pathways of social support. Again, within areas of social psychology and behavioral medicine, people are very interested in how friendships or being near others helps the progression of health or recovery from injury, disease, and other disruptive experiences.

This has been treated as if it were just an issue of—we'll give people social support. That's not the real issue; the real issue is that appropriate social interactions are actually using the same neural pathways that support health, growth, and restoration. When a sick person is moved into an environment where that person doesn't feel safe, you're doing something harmful, not helpful. So, the bottom line is the understanding that the human nervous system, like other mammalian species, is on a quest, and the quest is for safety, and we use others to help us feel safe.

HOW WE USE OTHERS TO FEEL SAFE

Dr. Buczynski: There is some research from maybe three or four years ago where they were looking at failing-practice physicians, and they recruited a whole bunch of people who were sick and randomly assigned them. Half got a warm connection and empathic listening to their symptoms; the other half got status quo medical treatment with no warmth and kindness. They found that the people who got the warmth and kindness recovered from the flu faster.

Dr. Porges: This makes physiological sense, and it's missing from our understanding of health care.

Dr. Buczynski: Why does it make physiological sense?

Dr. Porges: It makes sense because of the impact of social behavior on physiological state—the state of our autonomic nervous system. The cues from the safe individual enable the sick or compromised person not to be in defensive states. When we are in a defensive state, then we are using metabolic resources to defend. It's not merely that we can't be creative or loving when we're scared; we can't heal.

The neural pathway for healing overlaps with the neural pathway for social engagement. To be more specific, this is a vagal pathway that conveys information from the brain to the periphery. It is signaling safety to your body and calming you down.

If the higher-order parts of our nervous system detect risk or danger, then this vagal calming response is retracted and we become prepared for fight/flight behaviors. This occurs through an older phylogenetic circuit, the sympathetic nervous system, that enables defense to occur through mobilization.

Polyvagal Theory informs us that the phylogenetically newest vagal circuit is available only when the body detects features of safety. In addition to calming our visceral state, this circuit enables the face to work; our face can be expressive and our voice can be prosodic. When these features are projected from others, our body calms and our voice and face express positive affect.

Our temporal cortex reads this information as it is projected in the voice and face of others. This area of the brain detects biological movement and reflexively interprets intentionality. If you put a hand over the back of the head of a strange dog, what will happen? The dog may snap at you and attempt to bite you. If you put your hand down in front of the dog, the dog will sniff the hand and interpret your movement as a neutral engagement behavior and not get defensive. The temporal cortex contributes to the interpretation of facial expressivity, intonation, and gesture. This interpretative process leads to a 'neural' decision that is not cognitive as to whether the features of the engagement are safe or dangerous.

Dr. Buczynski: What about people who don't have the ability to read those?

Dr. Porges: Polyvagal Theory informs us that the inability to read these cues is a function of physiological state. Functionally, if a person is mobilized and in a defensive state, it will be difficult for them to detect cues of safety. If a person is "shut down" or dissociated, it will be almost impossible for them to detect cues of safety.

I want to expand this answer and discuss why the Polyvagal Theory evolved. Scientists have understood that there are fight/flight systems and they understood that there are calming systems, but they didn't understand that the calming system, involving the highly evolved mammalian vagus, was linked to the neural regulation of the muscles of the face and head. That's an important contribution by the Polyvagal Theory, and it's also important to understand that the autonomic nervous system predictably reacts as a hierarchy in which the uniquely mammalian vagal system could dampen the sympathetic nervous system. But what was missing or minimized in the literature, was an ancient and old defensive system of shutting down—death feigning—just as the mouse responds in the jaws of the cat.

Through our education and culture, we have been structured to think that humans have only one defense system, a system that increases mobilization and is expressed as fight/flight behaviors. Even our vocabulary limits our ability to understand defense, and we frequently use the word "stress" when our body is in a highly mobilized state of defense.

How do traumatized individuals describe their reactions? If you are stressed, your heart is beating rapidly and you feel tense. But these features are not always described by individuals who have experienced trauma and abuse. When survivors of trauma are interviewed, they often describe their personal experiences to the trauma and abuse as shutting down, losing muscle tone, losing consciousness, and dissociating.

Often when they described these features to their clinicians, the clinicians assumed that the client experience the trauma in a state of stress characterized by activation of the sympathetic nervous system and the associated fight/flight behaviors. This mismatch between the client's experience and the therapist's interpretation can disrupt the therapeutic experience with the client feeling that the therapist was not listening or understanding the client's personal narrative. This is why people who have experienced severe abuse and trauma often have difficulty explaining their experiences. They have a problem because clinicians, friends, and family often don't have the concept of an immobilization defensive system in their vocabulary.

When we talk about psychobiological treatments or we talk about basic models of stress and fear, people ask, "Are you studying fear?" I say, "Do you mean fear as in when we run away? Or fear as in when we pass out?"

We use psychological constructs, and those psychological constructs do not map well into biological adaptive responses. The reason that I am talking with you now is that people within the trauma field found that the Polyvagal Theory explained several important features of their clients. Before the Polyvagal Theory, they had no explanation of some the features their clients reported.

I was shocked that my ideas, which started with the explanation of bradycardia and apnea in babies, could be translated into the human experience of abuse and trauma. I am pleased that clinicians and clients are using Polyvagal Theory to validate personal narratives of how the body responds to trauma in a heroic manner. They are learning that their body responded in an adaptive way that enabled them to survive.

THREE SYSTEMS INFLUENCE HOW WE RESPOND TO THE WORLD

From my perspective, one of the major contributions of the Polyvagal Theory is the articulation that there are three components of the autonomic nervous system that are hierarchically organized to respond sequentially to challenges.

When we are in safe environments, we efficiently detect cues. We instantaneously process facial expressions, gestures, and vocal prosody. We need to emphasize the importance of a safe environment as a facilitator of these abilities. Sitting in an enclosed environment as we both are—you are in a room with four walls and a door and I'm in a room with four walls and a door—neither of us is concerned about what is happening behind us, and we are not turning our gaze from each other to check for a potential unknown and unsuspected danger. If we were conducting this interview in an open area, our nervous systems would constantly want to look behind us; we would want to identify potential risks.

But there are no risks in our rooms. We have created within our society environments that are defined as safe, because they have a certain amount of structure and predictability. We know that our nervous system wants this; we know that if we can use face-to-face interactions, we can diffuse many misinterpretations of events. Thus, face-to-face interactions are often very helpful in dampening and resolving conflict, especially if the interactions occur in a safe environment.

We also know that our sympathetic nervous system is really not a bad thing. We appreciate it as an enabler of movement, alertness, and exuberance. But if it is used primarily as a defense system, we become dangerous to others and ourselves. When our autonomic state is overwhelmed by our sympathetic nervous system, we in a sense become skittish. We'll aggressively hit others, and we'll misinterpret others' cues. Polyvagal Theory informs us that when the sympathetic nervous system is unrestrained by the myelinated (mammalian) vagal circuit, it becomes a defense system that can disrupt attempts to interact.

But there is another defense system, and that system is the shutdown system, which also has adaptive functions. It raises pain thresholds. It enables an individual to experience horrendous exposure to abuse and not consciously feel it and, thus, to survive.

But there are consequences of that survival strategy. Although mammals evolved to rapidly shift between the social engagement safe state and mobilization associated with activation of the sympathetic nervous system, we did not evolve to shift efficiently between shutting down and mobilization and between shutting down and social engagement.

If you think in terms of people who have been abused, their active defenses, if they can recruit them, are to flail out at people or try to escape from where they are. It is useful to think in terms of a response hierarchy, with each circuit having an adaptive function—each circuit having a useful purpose.

There is a problem when we use the immobilization circuit for defense, since our nervous system doesn't have an efficient pathway to get out of it. Many people are in therapy because they can't get out of the immobilization circuit.

THE VAGAL PARADOX

The vagus nerve is involved in shutting down (e.g., fainting, bradycardia, apnea), but it also is involved in social engagement and calming. Actually, the functions of the vagus nerve are paradoxical. The Polyvagal Theory was the product of trying to resolve this paradox.

How can these two processes occur via the same nerve? Can we speculate that this represents when too much of a good thing is bad? This speculation did not make sense to me because of observations in my research with human newborns. I observed bradycardia only in the absence of background heart rate variability. This was perplexing since both the bradycardia and heart rate variability were assumed to be mediated through vagal pathways.

Without robust heart rate variability patterns, bradycardia occurred. This observation sent me into an intellectual quandary. In a sense, being a scientist is a wonderful profession not because of what we know, but because of what we *don't* know.

Science is driven by questions, and questions can be structured into testable hypotheses.

In this case, the paradoxical functions of the vagus were understood by studying the evolutionary changes in how neural regulation of the heart, or more specifically how the function of the vagus, changed as vertebrates evolved. It is an interesting story, and, as research continues in several fields, the story is still developing. One might think the study of evolutionary changes in the neural systems regulating autonomic function would put someone to sleep, but it's exciting to identify neural changes in the phylogenetic transition from the primitive, now-extinct reptiles to mammals. Our ancient common ancestor probably had an autonomic nervous system similar to a turtle. What is the primary defense system of a turtle? Shutting down and even retracting the head!

Mammals inherited this ancient neural shutdown system. It's embedded in our nervous system. We don't use it often, and when we do, it has several risks. As mammals, we need lots of oxygen, so slowing our heart rate and stopping our breathing is not a good thing. However, if mobilization doesn't get us out of danger, our nervous system may automatically switch to this system.

The issue, again, is to understand that the physiological circuits or states we may experience are not voluntarily selected. Our nervous system is evaluating this on an unconscious level. I use the term neuroception to respect the role our nervous system has in reflexively evaluating features of risk in the environment.

If you start feeling comfortable with me and my voice has positive prosodic features; my gestures are inviting; I'm not yelling at you; I'm not talking in a deep tone of voice; I'm not lecturing you or forcing you to accept information. If I follow this sequence, you're going to start listening better and you're going to calm down. If I talk like most university professors, your eyes will start rolling up, and you'll lose interest and say that I made a good decision *not* to become a clinician!

We understand that when we spend more time with ideas and interacting with objects and not people, our ability to relate and interact with people may change. I will bridge these thoughts in a moment. But first, I want to emphasize that Polyvagal Theory uses evolution as an organizing principle to decipher and understand the neurophysiological circuits that regulate biobehavioral state.

Phylogenetically earlier vertebrates had only an unmyelinated vagus, which is a less efficient regulator of physiological state than a myelinated vagus. This unmyelinated vagal circuit provided ancient vertebrates with an ability to defend by immobilizing, which meant reducing metabolic demands, reducing oxygen demands, and reducing food demands.

As vertebrates evolved, a spinal sympathetic nervous system emerged in bony fish. This system supported movement, including the coordinated movement among groups, such as schools of fish. When highly activated, this mobilization system becomes a defense system and inhibits the immobilization circuit.

As mammals evolved, there were changes in the vagus. Mammals have a vagal pathway that differs from their evolutionary ancestors. This new vagal circuit had the capacity to dampen the sympathetic nervous system. By actively inhibiting the sympathetic nervous system, the mammalian vagus could down-regulate fight/flight defenses sufficiently to enable social engagement behaviors to spontaneously occur while optimizing metabolic resources and homeostatic processes. When we are social and are engaged, we are reducing metabolic demands to facilitate health, growth, and restoration.

There is another important issue. When the calming vagus emerged in mammals, the area of the brainstem that regulated the newer myelinated vagus was linked to the brainstem areas that controlled the muscles of the face and head. This brainstem area controls our ability to listen through middle ear muscles, our ability to articulate through the laryngeal-pharyngeal muscles, and our ability to express emotion and intention through the face.

As a clinical psychologist, when you look at clients' faces and listen to their voices, you are inferring information about their physiological state because the face and heart are wired together in the brainstem. Again, an important clinical observation, especially in treating individuals with trauma, is the covariation of an emotionally flat upper face with a voice that lacks prosody. When these features occur, the client may also have difficulties understanding human voice in background sound while being hypersensitive to background noises.

When we listen to intonation—prosodic features of voice—we are reading the other person's physiological state. If the physiological state is calm, it is reflected in a melodic voice, and listening to that voice calms us down. Another way of thinking about the relation between vocalizations and listening is to understand that long before there was syntax or language in mammals, there were vocalizations, and vocalizations were an important component of social interaction. Vocalizations convey to conspecifics—members of the same species—whether that individual is dangerous or safe to come close to.

THE VAGUS: A CONDUIT OF MOTOR AND SENSORY PATHWAYS

Dr. Buczynski: Is the vagus nerve a family of nerves or a neural pathway that originates in several areas of the brainstem?

Dr. Porges: There are two ways of looking at this. You can ask the question: Where does the vagus nerve come from? Or you can ask: Where does the vagus nerve go to?

The vagal motor fibers going from the brain to the visceral organs and vagal sensory fibers coming to the brainstem are located in different areas, although they exit the brain in a common nerve that functions more as a conduit. Think of the vagus as a conduit, a cable with lots of fibers in it. The vagus is not merely a motor nerve, meaning that it comes from the brain to the viscera; it's also a sensory nerve, going from the viscera up to the brain.

Now you have the neural pathways to explain many of the mind–body, body–mind, or brain–body, body–brain relationships. Eighty percent of the fibers in the vagus are sensory. Only approximately one in six of the motor fibers are myelinated. The few myelinated vagal motor fibers are profoundly important in providing the primary vagal motor input to the organs above the diaphragm. Most of the unmyelinated vagal pathways regulate organs below the diaphragm.

There are three vagal pathways, consisting of sensory fibers and two types of motor fibers—motor fibers traveling through the unmyelinated vagus going primarily below the diaphragm (i.e., subdiaphragrmatic vagus) to organs such as the gut, and motor fibers through the myelinated vagus going primarily above the diaphragm (i.e, supradiaphragmatic vagus) to organs such as the heart. In the brainstem the sensory fibers terminate in an area known as nucleus of the solitary track, the myelinated vagal motor pathways originate primarily in the nucleus ambiguus, and the unmyelinated vagal motor pathways originate primarily in the dorsal nucleus of the vagus.

To link these pathways to clinical features, think about the health and behavioral problems of your clients. They may have gut and gastric problems, which may be the product of the unmyelinated vagus being recruited as an immobilization defense system. Subdiaphragmatic problems can also occur when the individual uses the mobilized fight/flight defense system chronically. When this occurs, the activated sympathetic nervous system dampens the ability of the unmyelinated vagus to support homeostatic functions including digestion.

Dr. Buczynski: Polyvagal hierarchy states that there are different zones of arousal affected by trauma. Is that correct?

Dr. Porges: The theory functionally states that if you are confronted with a challenge, based on evolution, the most recent part of your nervous system will attempt to negotiate safety by using the face and vocalizations. If that doesn't work, the social engagement system will be withdrawn including the vagal inhibition on the heart (i.e., vagal brake), which would increase heart rate to promote mobilization in anticipation of defending with fight/flight behaviors. If that doesn't work, then you're going to ramp up the sympathetic nervous system for fight/flight.

If you can't escape or fight, then you may reflexively shut down. This is a feature of many trauma narratives, especially with small children and other situations in which there is a size differential or if the survivor is confronted with an assailant with a weapon.

Basically, signals of risk may be translated by different neural circuits into different physiological states and behaviors. These variations in responses to a common signal or event leads to one the most difficult problems in treating trauma. Trauma treatment and diagnosis have been focused and biased on the event and not on understanding that an individual's response to the event is the critical feature.

THE CONNECTION BETWEEN TRAUMA AND SOCIAL ENGAGEMENT

The critical point is that if people go into a state of immobilization with fear, they are using a very ancient neural circuit. Through evolution, the human nervous system has been modified, and these modifications appear to hamper the ability to easily transition out of the immobilization-with-fear state back to a safety state characterized by spontaneous social engagement behaviors.

When stuck in states that do not promote social interaction and a sense of safety, individuals develop complex narratives of why they don't want to socially interact and why they don't trust others. There narratives provide an interpretation of their visceral physiological feelings. Their nervous system is detecting risk when there is no real risk, and their narrative provides their justification for not being loving, trusting, and spontaneously engaging.

When this occurs, how do you get a person out of that loop of defense and justification? How do you recruit the social engagement system and inhibit both the sympathetic mobilization fight/flight state and enable the person to come out of the dangerous immobilization shutdown state? In response to this question, insights from the Polyvagal Theory are moving into the clinical world.

From the Polyvagal perspective, first the client needs to negotiate and navigate in any environment to experience a physiological state of *safety*. Often it has to do with the proximity to the therapist. In a sense, the client with a trauma history may react to the therapist as dangerous. The clinician needs to empower the client to navigate and negotiate in both physical and psychological space until the client feels safe. Once the client feels safe, there will be a concomitant shift in the client's physiological state. When this occurs, spontaneous engagement behaviors will emerge with changes in voice and facial affect.

I suggest two points to clinicians. First, empower the client to negotiate safety. Second, understand the principles of neuroception that enable us to understand that the nervous system, in safe environments, will respond to certain features differently than it will in dangerous situations.

Since noisy environments that contain low-frequency sounds are triggers of predator to our nervous system, removing low-frequency sounds and background noise will optimize the healing potential of the clinical space. It is important for the clinical space to be relatively quiet. Many clients with a trauma history are extremely uncomfortable in public places. Often they don't want to go to restaurants or movie theaters. When they walk in shopping malls, they feel threatened and overwhelmed by sounds, vibrations, and proximity to others. The low-frequency sounds and vibrations from the escalators bother them. If we know this, why don't we create environments where they will feel safer?

Once the client feels safe, the therapeutic strategy may

proceed efficiently. But how would we trigger the social engagement system to ensure that the client is feeling safe? Some options are wired into our nervous system. For example, listening to the prosodic features of sound, such as listening to vocal music even without another person, may make us feel safer.

HOW MUSIC CUES VAGAL REGULATION

Listening to vocal music was part of an intervention that I developed. The Listening Project Protocol (see Chapter 2) was initially implemented with autistic individuals. The intervention exercises the neural regulation of the middle ear muscles by exaggerating the processing intonation of voice, and that feeds back as a cue to a nervous system that they are in a safe place, which changes that vagal regulation of the heart.

Dr. Buczynski: What do you do in the music project?

Dr. Porges: I computer-alter vocal music. Vocal music, especially female vocal music, uses intonation without low frequencies. The computer processing of the vocal music emphasizes and functionally amplifies the modulations. This is equivalent to exaggerating prosody, which would efficiently trigger the neural circuit that detects and responds to prosodic voices.

The intervention was theoretically designed to trigger the neural circuits that detect prosody, which trigger descending neural pathways that would increase the neural tone to the middle ear muscles to dampen background sounds and improve the ability to understand human voices. Since the brainstem areas regulating the middle ear muscles are also involved in regulating facial expressivity, prosodic vocalizations, and vagal influences to the heart, the listening intervention was designed to stimulate the integrated social engagement system.

For 15 years, I had a plausible hypothesis, derived from the Polyvagal Theory, that linked the neural regulation of middle ear structures to hyperacusis and auditory processing. Specifically, I hypothesized that shifts in the neural regulation of middle ear muscles would deterministically shift the transfer function of middle ear structures providing a plausible mechanism explaining why auditory hypersensitivity covaried with difficulties in the processing of human speech. However, although the Listening Project Protocol reduced both auditory hypersensitivities and improved auditory processing, there was no device or test available to measure the transfer function of the middle ear and test this hypothesis. This problem was solved by my former graduate student, Greg Lewis. By 2011, Greg Lewis had finished his PhD research in my laboratory, in which he developed a device that measured the transfer function to middle ear structures. It was a concept that was missing from speech and hearing sciences. We call the device the Middle Ear Sound Absorption System, or MESAS (Porges & Lewis, 2011).

Now we are able to objectively evaluate which sounds pass into the brain or are bouncing off the eardrum. MESAS (see Chapter 2) documents whether people are absorbing human voice through their eardrum or whether these sounds are being masked by absorbing the low-frequency sounds that our nervous system interprets as predator sounds. Visualize the eardrum as a kettledrum. When the skin on the kettledrum is tightened, the pitch goes up, meaning that higher frequencies are selectively absorbed and lower frequencies are not.

MESAS provides an objective measure of auditory hypersensitivity. We have tested MESAS with several children with a diagnosis of autism. We also have tested others with a history of trauma, who frequently report auditory hypersensitivities. In preliminary research, we documented that the absorption in the frequency band of the human voice was diminished, especially in the frequency band of the second and third formants of human voice. Formants are concentrations of acoustic energy at specific frequencies that correspond to resonance frequencies of the vocal tract. People with auditory hyperacusis absorb more of the low frequencies, while the higher-order formants that enable us to distinguish various vocal sounds are distorted. The ability to process these higher-order formants contributes to an ability to distinguish consonants and to process the ends of words.

We tested several of our participants before and after the Listening Project Protocol. In a subset of these participants, middle ear transfer function was normalized. This meant that in some of our participants we were able to rehabilitate the neural regulation of the middle ear muscles. MESAS provided documentation of a change in the sound absorption curve, meaning that more of the frequencies associated with human speech were absorbed. Before these observations, clinicians assumed that hyperacusis and difficulties in auditory processing were determined by neural circuits located in the cortex. They did not understand the role of the middle ear structures as a filter nor its role in the social engagement system, which linked auditory processing and hyperacusis to difficulties in behavioral state regulation and other features of the social engagement system.

About 50 percent of the participants in our Listening Project Protocol studies, who entered the study with auditory hypersensitivities, no longer had auditory hypersensitivities after the intervention (Porges et al., 2014). Most of this subset of participants also had improved social engagement behaviors. In another study, we documented that the improved social engagement behaviors were paralleled by an increase in vagal regulation of autonomic state, supporting the plausible hypothesis that changing autonomic state with the intervention functionally changes the neural platform for social engagement behaviors, reducing defensive behaviors (Porges et al., 2013).

Dr. Buczynski: How about music therapy? Does that have any effect?

Dr. Porges: Yes. There are two parts of music therapy that would be very helpful to many individuals. The issue with music therapy is that the mechanisms through which it works are not understood. Although there are positive reports, there is no real strong theory of why or how it works. However, the Polyvagal Theory with its linkage to the middle-ear muscles and linkage to laryngeal and pharyngeal muscles, which are involved in singing, could be used to explain how it works and why it would be beneficial.

When people sing, they control their breath. The process of singing requires expanding the duration of exhalation. During the exhalation phase of breathing, there is an increase in the effectiveness of the myelinated vagal efferent pathways on the heart. This explains how singing or playing a wind instrument would contribute to a calmer physiological state and provide greater access to the social engagement system.

Singing is more than just exhaling. What else do you do when you sing? You listen and this increases the neural tone of your middle ear muscles. What else do you do? You utilize the neural regulation of your laryngeal and pharyngeal muscles. What else do you do? You utilize the muscles of your mouth and face through the facial and trigeminal nerves.

If you sing with a group, then you're social referencing—you're engaging others. So singing, especially singing in a group, is an amazing neural exercise of the social engagement system.

Playing a wind instrument is very similar and involves listening, exhaling, and engaging whoever is leading or conducting the music.

Pranayama yoga is another strategy that employs similar processes. Pranayama yoga, functionally, is yoga of the social engagement system—yoga of breath and of the striated muscles of the face and head.

SOCIAL ENGAGEMENT SIGNALS: SELF-REGULATION VERSUS "HAVING NO CLUE"

Dr. Buczynski: Awhile back, we were talking about why some people need those social engagement signals and other people just have no clue—as if it's a foreign language and they've just immigrated to a foreign country.

Dr. Porges:. Let's start off by forgetting that we have all these complex diagnostic categories. If we use diagnostic categories, we end up describing comorbidities and using other terms that are not helpful in understanding the underlying functions and processes.

Let's create a very simple model of human behavior. Let's rank people based on their ability to co-regulate with other individuals along a continuum. This is really what you're saying: Some people don't have a clue about other people's features, and what it's telling you is that their ability to co-regulate their physiological state is really not good with other people.

Now, let's create another dimension. Let's ask about people who self-regulate with objects. Remember that in our contemporary society, technologies for social communication are literally being pushed on us by people who are challenged in terms of their own social communication skills and their ability to co-regulate with others. We label this new technology social networking. We use computers. We text with a smartphone. In a sense, we are stripping the essence of human interactions, direct face-to-face experiences, from human interactions. We're moving from a synchronous interactive strategy to an asynchronous one in which we leave messages and look at people later. We are allowing the world to be organized based upon principles of individuals who have difficulty regulating their biobehavioral state in the presence of others but who may regulate well with objects.

In a very global clinical perspective, many of the disorders that therapists are actively requested to treat are about difficulties regulating state with others. When individuals have difficulty regulating state with others or co-regulating, they adaptively gravitate to regulating state with objects.

Sometimes these tendencies lead to clinical labels. Whether it is labeled autism or social anxieties doesn't really matter. What we know is that these individuals' nervous systems are not enabled to engage in reciprocal social interactions. It is rare for them to feel safe with people and get into that, beneficial physiological states that enable social behavior to support health, growth, and restoration. For these people, social behavior is disruptive and not supportive. Individuals may self-select into two different groups that are categorized by either regulating through social interaction or through the use of objects.

A secondary problem is the impact of these two strategies on the education and the socialization of children. Changes in education are moving away from face-to-face interactions. Schools now are putting iPads in the hands of preschoolers and elementary school children. I was watching a recent newscast of a school in which iPads were being used in elementary school. The school officials were extremely proud of this decision to embrace this technology. When the camera scanned the classroom, the children were looking at the iPads and not looking at each other or at the teacher.

What does this really mean? It means that the nervous system is not having the opportunity to exercise the neural regulatory circuits associated with social engagement behaviors. Without opportunities to exercise these neural circuits, children will not develop the natural capacity to self-regulate and regulate with others when challenged.

Another important point here is what happens to the school systems. Under the pressure in our cognitive-centric, cortical-centric world, we are bombarded with an increasing amount of information without understanding that our nervous system needs to be in a physiological state regulated by the myelinated vagus to process information sufficiently to generate new bold ideas, to be creative, and to experience positive social behavior. Rather than enabling these expansive and positive attributes of the nervous system with group behaviors requiring co-regulation such as singing in a choir, playing a musical instrument in an orchestra, or physically playing with another during recess—all opportunities to exercise the social engagement system and the myelinated vagal pathway—we misinterpret these opportunities for neural exercise as distracters from the opportunity to sit longer in the classroom. The students get more information, of course, but the information is not being efficiently processed, and oppositional behaviors are popping up. It's a naive view of the educational process and human development.

I think this line of inquiry should lead to questions about early experience, the consequences of those early experiences, and how early experiences may lead to other risk factors. We should approach these questions from neural, developmental, and even exercise models. For example, if we don't use specific neural circuits in regulating behavior and physiology, they will not develop well. It doesn't mean that we are so pessimistic that we can't recruit them later; it means that because we haven't recruited them early, there are going to be consequences.

RECRUITING NEURAL REGULATION

Dr. Buczynski: How do we help someone who hasn't recruited them learn how to recruit them?

Dr. Porges: The first thing, of course, is the context of safety. I was going to say depending upon the age of the client, but actually, regardless of age, the first thing is to convey to the client that they did not do anything wrong. As soon as we ask a client to change, the client often interprets this to mean that they did something wrong. Once this "critical" feedback is processed by the nervous system, the nervous system might switch into a state of defense, which will make it more difficult for the client to understand and maintain a calm state. So, there's a total paradox between how our nervous system functions and how we raise our children, teach our students, and treat our clients.

If we want individuals to feel safe, we don't accuse them of doing something wrong or bad. We explain to them how their body responded, how their responses are adaptive, how we need to appreciate this adaptive feature, and how the client needs to understand that this adaptive feature is flexible and can change in different contexts. Then we can use our wonderfully creative and integrative brain to develop a narrative that treats our atypical behaviors not as bad, but as understandable in terms of adaptive functions that may often be heroic.

HOW ATTACHMENT THEORY CONNECTS TO ADAPTIVE FUNCTION

Dr. Buczynski: How does attachment connect to the Polyvagal Theory?

Dr. Porges: This is a frequently asked question and the answer is partially linked to Sue Carter's research. Sue is both my colleague and wife. Sue discovered the relationship between oxytocin and social bonding. For several years, I would say that the study of social behavior, including social bonding and attachment, was her research area and not mine. She developed her ideas about social bonding by observing and conducting research with the prairie vole, a small rodent with very interesting social behavior, including pair-bonding for life and a parenting style in which father and mother share in the care of their offspring. The vole is quite an amazing animal.

The prairie vole has a high level of oxytocin, and for the past few years, we've been doing research together in which we measure in the vole vagal regulation of the heart. This small mammal, weighing approximately 50 grams, has vagal regulation of the heart at levels very similar to humans, which is very atypical for rodents and small mammals.

Since I started to collaborate with Sue, I have started to feel more comfortable discussing social behavior, including the area of attachment. But as we started to collaborate, I realized that an important setting condition leading to attachment was missing in the attachment literature. Missing is what I called the preamble to attachment, and the preamble to attachment is dependent on the signals of safety. I felt that one couldn't discuss issues of attachment without discussing safety and the features of social engagement. From my perspective, the social engagement system with the myelinated vagal pathway provides the neural platform upon which attachment processes can occur. It's a hierarchy. First safety, then healthy attachment would naturally follow.

Sue and I having been working on a concept that we call the neural love code. The love code has two parts: Phase one is social engagement, which uses cues of safety via engagement behaviors to negotiate proximity. Phase two deals with physical contact and intimacy. To articulate this as a code would mean that if the two processes do not occur in the right order, there would be problems associated with attachment and bonding.

I think, from a clinical perspective, that people bonding to each other without feeling safe with each other can be one of the driving forces for couples to come to therapy. The point I am emphasizing is that attachment should not be discussed on any level, whether it is theoretical or practical, without a thorough understanding of the setting—the conditions of safety and social engagement.

MAKING HOSPITALS MORE PSYCHOLOGICALLY SAFE

Dr. Buczynski: I want to ask you about hospitals and making hospitals more psychologically safe. Hospitalization is a time when we would hope that our facilities and the way we organize them would enhance healing processes and the immune system functioning. But I'm not sure that we are the best at that because we're focusing so much on other things.

Dr. Porges: I think this is an important question, and of course the answer is that very little effort has gone into this. Those of us who have been hospitalized can tell you the situation of being awakened every hour, dressed in a revealing gown, and the chronic noises that provide a continuous signal to your body to get out of the hospital because the hospital is not safe.

The issue has a lot to do with who organizes hospitals and sets their agenda. What are the goals of hospitals and their staffs? They are there to deliver health services to patients and to protect staff from being sued for malpractice. Within this agenda, health surveillance and cleanliness are prioritized. Other issues such as social support tend not to be treated as important, which is tragic.

When we are admitted into a hospital, our nervous system functionally informs us with cues that trigger thoughts consistent with the narrative: "I'm going into a physical situation where I cannot protect myself. I want to be assured that I'm in safe, loving hands." Unfortunately, most patients do not feel safe in hospitals.

I think it is really tragic, because there are so many well trained and loving clinicians in medical and allied health areas who could create a different type of clinical setting for people going into hospitals.

Rather than being overwhelmed with documents to sign that release the hospital from legal responsibilities—because you can't get the service unless you sign—why not have someone who functions like a concierge for your body to help you navigate through the hospital? This person could take you to the hospital and take the burden of hypervigilance from you. With these burdens and uncertainties removed, your body could be a willing collaborator with the medical treatments instead of frightened and locked in a state of defense.

The issue, as we discussed very early in the interview, is that if you're frightened and if you're scared, you're not going to heal efficiently. If we know this, why don't we do whatever we can to make people feel safe?

We need to realize that as human beings, we require reciprocity and feeling safe.

Dr. Buczynski: Before we close, I just wanted to ask you, Stephen, what's next for you?

Dr. Porges: I think of myself as a mature scientist who has done some interesting research, and I intend to do many more new interesting things. I intend to continue working to translate my basic research into clinical practice. For example, rather than thinking that medical treatments can only be surgical or pharmaceutical, we will be developing interventions that recruit the neural circuits that support health, growth, and restoration.

4

HOW POLYVAGAL THEORY EXPLAINS THE CONSEQUENCES OF TRAUMA ON BRAIN, BODY, AND BEHAVIOR

Stephen W. Porges and Ruth Buczynski

THE ORIGINS OF POLYVAGAL THEORY

Dr. Buczynski: Today, we'll probably touch on how Polyvagal Theory connects to autism, borderline personality disorder, and many other behaviors and diagnoses. But it all starts with understanding the vagus nerve.

Dr. Porges: First let's outline the major features of the Polyvagal Theory.

Polyvagal Theory is based on the evolution of our autonomic nervous system. Due to evolution there's a big difference between the behavioral repertoire of our reptilian ancestors and our mammalian cousins. Mammals need to find social relationships, they need to be parented and protected, and they need to protect each other. Reptiles tend to be solitary—so the concept of social behavior is based on the behavioral adaptations that distinguish reptiles from mammals. With this transition through evolution, the autonomic nervous system changed in structure and function.

Our autonomic nervous system changed from a system that enabled our vertebrate ancestors to mobilize and to shut down, and could support two different types of defenses: One was to fight and flee, and the other was to immobilize, like many reptiles do. But with the evolution of mammals, a new component or branch of the autonomic nervous system emerged that basically functioned as a "cheerleader" to activate circuits and to act as a "conductor" to coordinate the functions of the two more primitive components. It enabled the primitive biobehavioral response systems of sympathetic fight/flight and vagal shutting-down to be synergistic and support health, growth, and restoration. But, this can only occur in safe situations.

Dr. Buczynski: Tell me a little bit about what you meant by "cheerleader" and "conductor."

Dr. Porges: The "conductor" is the easier one to start with because the new component of the autonomic nervous system is linked to neural structures that create social context and involve higher brain structures to inform the brainstem structures, which regulate the older portions of the autonomic nervous system not to be defensive and to support health, growth, and restoration. It's like we use our higher brain structures to detect danger—and if there is no danger, then we're functionally inhibiting older defense systems. The conductor is basically applying an evolutionaly determined hierarchy in which newer circuits regulate and control older circuits. This is how the brain is phylogenetically organized.

The autonomic nervous system contains structures that are

not solely in our viscera. This understanding of the autonomic nervous system acknowledges the importance of brainstem areas in which nerves regulating the structures of the autonomic nervous system originate and the importance of how higher brain structures, including the cortex, influence these brainstem areas.

We have our conductor, which is saying, "It's okay. Those systems don't need to be recruited for defense—they can be used synergistically to support health, growth and even pleasure."

Now, the "cheerleader" is the concept similar to the actions of a cheerleader at a football game. The cheerleader is mobilized but is keeping the mobilized behavior from being defensive by using facial expressivity and prosodic vocalizations, features of the social engagement system. The cheerleader role functionally uses mobilization, but not for defense. By integrating mobilization with the social engagement system, the same system that is involved in fight/flight is now involved in prosocial behavior, which we call "play."

The difference between fight/flight and play is that while mobilizing, we're making eye contact and engaging each other. We're diffusing the cues of threat with social cues, so we can utilize the sympathetic nervous system to support movement without moving into defensive fight/flight behaviors. When we involve the social engagement system, we can even use the oldest system, which is immobilization, and we can be in the arms of someone that we feel safe with.

That is the Polyvagal Theory. Let me unpack the name for you. The Polyvagal Theory uses "vagus" in the title, and polyvagal means "many vagi" or, more accurately, "many vagal pathways."—I created the title as a reminder that there has been a phylogenetic change, an evolutionary change in the neural regulation of the autonomic nervous system.

THE "VEGETATIVE VAGUS" AND THE "SMART VAGUS"

Dr. Buczynski: In your book, you talk about "two vagal motor systems"—the "vegetative vagus" associated with a more passive regulation of visceral functions, and then the "smart vagus."

Dr. Porges: There's a paradox that resides in studying the parasympathetic nervous system. The vagus is the major neural pathway of the parasympathetic nervous system. During most of our discussion, the vagus and the parasympathetic nervous system will be used interchangeably. However, to be more accurate, vagal pathways are only a subset of pathways in the parasympathetic nervous system. The parasympathetic nervous system, when you read the literature, is always associated with health, growth, and restoration—it is the "good guy."

The sympathetic is always presented as if it is the "mortal enemy" that we need to control. That is partially true, but this distinction really doesn't help us understand clinical conditions.

What happens if you're immobilized with fear and your heart stops through a vagal pathway, or you're immobilized with fear and you defecate through a vagal pathway, or you can't breathe because your bronchi constrict through a vagal pathway? We can't explain that as being "good."

So there was a real paradox in our understanding how the parasympathetic nervous system works, and that paradox was that virtually all the information regarding the involvement of the vagal pathway as part of a defense system was selectively expunged from general models of the autonomic nervous system. Again, if we look at reptiles their primary defense system: immobilization, inhibition of breathing, slowing up the heart rate—"death feigning"—basically fainting and looking like they are dead.

In fact, when we look at a mouse in the jaws of a cat, what are the mouse's features? The mouse's features are an apparent cessation of breathing, heart rate very slow, looking as if it were dead or dying. This is all involuntary, so if we assume that influences from the parasympathetic nervous system, through the vagus, are only positive, we are wrong!

This paradox triggered my interest. For more than 20 years, I worked to solve this problem. The problem was solved by understanding that through evolution, changes occurred in the neural regulation of the autonomic nervous system. Mapping the phylogenetic changes in neural regulation of the autonomic nervous system, we can see a second vagal pathway emerging as mammals evolved. We can see the same changes developmentally when we study fetal development in mammals.

When preterm babies are born, they're born without this new, smart, mammalian vagus, and what happens is that vagal responses can be deadly—and in the neonatal intensive care unit, these vagal responses produce apnea and bradycardia, when neonates stop breathing and their heart beats too slow.

However, many of us learned that vagal responses were "good" and supported health. But this is not true for the preterm, who does not have access to the newer myelinated vagus that becomes functional later in gestation. Functionally, the preterm infant, born before 32 weeks of gestation, is born with an autonomic nervous system with features of a reptile. The vulnerability to apnea and bradycardia are manifestations of reptilian defense reactions. Only in full-term newborns is the new myelinated vagus available to coordinate the other vagal circuit and the sympathetic nervous system to support homeostasis and health.

Dr. Buczynski: That is the "smart vagus."

Dr. Porges: Yes, and we can use interchangeable words: mammalian, smart, and myelinated to describe this uniquely mammalian vagal pathway.

This vagal pathway can be contrasted with a more vegetative, unmyelinated vagal pathway. We can make another distinction between the two vagal pathways: One vagus is primarily subdiaphragmatic and the other is primarily supradiaphragmatic.

The supradiaphragmatic vagus is primarily myelinated and goes to organs above the diaphragm, such as the heart and bronchi; the subdiaphragmatic is primarily unmyelinated and goes to organs below the diaphragm, such as the gut. The subdiaphragmatic is shared with reptiles, fish, amphibians—and it goes subdiaphragmatically, regulating our gut primarily. When we talk about clinical disorders, we talk about things "getting to our gut."

When describing vagal pathways that go above the diaphragm, we're really talking about the neural regulation of the heart and the bronchi. The vagal control to organs above the diaphragm is primarily through the myelinated vagus. When the myelinated vagal pathway loses control of the heart, then we may feel either the heart palpitating through the influence of the sympathetic nervous system or a massive slowing of heart rate through the influence of the unmyelinated vagus. Note that although the unmyelinated vagus is "primarily" regulating organs below the diaphragm, there are unmyelinated fibers that go to the heart and can cause bradycardia.

The cues of our body tell us a lot about this system. But let's incorporate the brain in our discussion, because each of these vagal pathways actually comes from a different area in the brainstem—and this is why Polyvagal Theory, by incorporating brain structures and functions, is more than a theory of a peripheral nerve.Although the vagus is a peripheral nerve, it originates in the brain and terminates in peripheral organs. However, both vagal pathways originate in different nuclei in the brainstem (i.e., nucleus ambiguus and dorsal nucleus of the vagus). The sensory pathways of the vagus terminate within a third nucleus in the brainstem (i.e., nucleus of the solitary tract).

An interesting and important point is that the smart, myelinated, mammalian vagus comes from an area of the brainstem that controls the muscles of the face and head. Well-socialized people and observant clinicians and educators are constantly looking at the people with whom they are interacting. When they look at the person, they often can tell how a person is feeling.

This ability to feel another's feelings is based on our neurophysiology. We can detect and interpret how another person feels, because the nerves that control the striated muscles of the face and head are linked in the brainstem to the myelinated smart vagus. We functionally wear our heart on our face. Our brains automatically interpret this information and our body responds. Although insightful clinicians intuitively know this, Polyvagal Theory explains the process.

As these processes evolved it enabled conspecifics, those of the same species, to detect whether it was safe to approach another. The cues of safety and threat are conveyed not only in the muscles of the face, but also with the muscles that control vocalization. If an approaching mammal is physiologically activated and prepared to be aggressive, these features of physiological state are reflected in their face and voice.

When we talk to a person on a phone, we may ask them if something is wrong, based on listening to the features of their voice. If their voice lacks prosody, when the voice is less modulated and more monotonic, we may become more concerned that something is wrong. Prosody is dependent on the neural regulation of the muscles of the larynx and pharynx, which is regulated in the area of the brainstem that regulates the myelinated vagus. In fact, myelinated vagal pathways are involved in the production of prosody, and these vagal pathways parallel the vagal regulation of the heart.

THE VAGUS NERVE: A FAMILY OF NEURAL PATHWAYS

Dr. Buczynski: Let's get to a couple more foundational questions before we move on. Biologically, I know, the vagus nerve is not just one nerve, but a family of neural pathways originating in several areas of the brainstem and going into several branches of the vagus.

Dr. Porges: The vagus is a cranial nerve that emerges from the brainstem. We have 12 cranial nerves, and some of these cranial nerves control the striated muscles of the face. In general, when neural control of muscles is discussed, the discussion focuses on skeletal muscles involved in moving the limbs of our body that are controlled by nerves emerging from the spinal cord. But cranial nerves are not the equivalent of spinal nerves regulating the striated muscles of the face and head. For example, facial expressivity is regulated by cranial nerves emerging from the brain and is distinct from the spinal regulation of the muscles of the trunk and limbs. In addition, the vagus is involved with the regulation of the striated muscles of the face and head, and it also regulates smooth and cardiac muscle.

Polyvagal Theory focuses on five cranial nerves that emerge from the brainstem. We can describe the brain as an inverted triangle with the expansive cortex at the top and a narrow brainstem at the base. Most research studying the brain, especially with imaging techniques, focuses on the cortex and tends to minimize and neglect the brainstem. However, from a parsimonious perspective, the brainstem is a final common pathway through which most information comes into the brain and leaves the brain. It is useful to think of the brainstem as a building block upon which other processes are scaffolded. If we can't regulate our physiological state, which is a brainstem responsibility, then we have difficulties accessing and processing higher cognitive functions.

The brainstem as an anatomical structure provides an opportunity to compare across vertebrate species and to infer the adaptive modifications that occurred during evolution. Functionally, the brainstem is the major regulator of physiological state. Since the regulation of physiological state prepares us for a range of behaviors, the brainstem is critical in all aspects of our behavior as well as in the maintenance of homeostatic processes that keep us alive and healthy.

A major clinical issue manifested across diagnostic categories is difficulty in behavioral state regulation. Polyvagal Theory assumes that difficulties in behavioral state regulation are manifestations of difficulties in autonomic regulation. The ability to regulate behavioral state is a clinically relevant process when discussing borderline, schizophrenia, depression, anxiety, autism, and other clinical disorders. The ability to regulate state, when context and demands dynamically change, is frequently used to operationalize resilience.

To understand the relevance of the Polyvagal Theory to clinical conditions, it is necessary to think of the vagus as a bidirectional conduit connecting the brain with the body. The vagal conduit has motor pathways going from the brain to the organs and sensory pathways coming from the organs to the brain. Polyvagal Theory is about the brain–body communication that involves the vagus. The theory forces us to see the function of peripheral organs as impacting on brain processes and brain processes as impacting on visceral organs. Polyvagal Theory enables us to reconceptualize the regulation of visceral organs and forces us to stop thinking of our organs as independent structures floating in a visceral sea unconnected and uninformed by brain processes.

Vagal fibers originate and terminate in different areas of the brainstem and have different responsibilities. Some come from the brain and go to specific visceral organs, but many fibers come from the visceral organs to the brain. This sensory system serves a surveillance function to help maintain optimal regulation of visceral organs. About 80 percent of the vagal fibers are sensory, and those sensory ones have tremendous impact on the accessibility of certain brain structures.

Polyvagal theory emphasizes that the vagus changed with evolution. One of these modifications occurred during the emergence of mammals. In mammals, the brainstem regulation of some of the vagal pathways became integrated with the regulation of the face. This resulted in features of our physiological state being expressed in our face and voice. The adaptive function of this modification is obvious; as a mammal, we don't want to engage another mammal if that mammal is in a physiological state of rage.

It we get close to another conspecific in a physiological state that supports rage and we encroach into their personal space, they will become defensive. In mammals, this behavioral strategy will be expressed by attempts to fight off the intruder by growling, hissing, scratching, and biting. We don't want to be injured. We want to recieve the signal that it's okay to come close. Mammals convey this information through facial expression and through prosodic features of vocalizations. The muscles regulating those functions are linked to the myelinated vagus that regulates the heart. These signals of safety are wired into our nervous system.

This linkage between the vagal regulation of the heart and the regulation of the muscles of the face and head enables us to see indices of physiological state in faces and hear physiological state in voices. In addition, when there is a down-regulation of muscle tone in the face and head, the middle ear muscles lose their neural tone and become hypersensitive to the low-frequency sounds associated with predator. With this shift in middle ear function, it becomes difficult to extract the meaning of human voice, since it is necessary to hear relatively soft, high-frequency harmonics to understand speech.

Research documents that several clinical disorders are associated with both a reduction in vagal regulation of the heart and a dampening of the neural regulation of muscles of the face and head. This dampening of the muscles of the face and head is manifested in flat affect, lack of vocal prosody, auditory hypersensitivities, and difficulty in understanding verbal instructions. Collectively, as we have mentioned earlier, the face-heart system forms an integrated social engagement system, which is functionally dampened in several disorders projecting a flat affect, with an underlying depression of vagal regulation and lowered threshold to trigger the sympathetic activation required for fight/flight behaviors. When this system is dampened early in life, it can contribute to difficulties in language development.

Let's link these processes related to atypical vagal function and state regulation to clinical disorders. Rather than using standardized psychiatric disorder-specific diagnostic systems, we could ask what common features are shared with several clinical disorders.

If we take this approach, we find that state regulation—the ability to regulate behavioral state—is a basic problem shared with several diagnostic categories. We also find that, coupled with observable disruptions of behavioral-state regulation, other features related to the neuromuscular control of the face would be manifested. The upper part of the face would appear unresponsive, similar to the effects of Botox. The orbital muscle around the eye, called the orbicularis oculi, is controlled by a branch of the facial nerve. The facial nerve is also a cranial nerve. This branch of the facial nerve is also involved in regulating the neural tone to the stapedius, a small muscle in the middle ear. When this muscle loses its tension, a person will have auditory hypersensitivities and have difficulty extracting voice from background sound (Borg & Counter, 1989).

The middle ear muscles control the smallest bones in our body. They influence what happens to the energy of sounds that hit our eardrum and get transmitted into the inner ear and then to our brain. When the middle ear muscles aren't contracting appropriately, we are bombarded with low-frequency rumble from background sound. This compromises our ability to understand human voices. When this occurs, the adaptive behavior is to move oneself from the source of the sounds, and this results in those with sound sensitivities withdrawing from social settings.

I want to emphasize that the cues conveyed by our voice and face are really manifestations of our physiology, what's going on in our body. These cues convey to the other individual whether we are safe to approach. This ability to cue and to detect these cues is embedded in our physiology and is part of the evolutionary history of mammals.

In my laboratory, we looked at the acoustic features of infant cries and their heart rate and found significant correlations (Stewart et al., 2013). The higher-pitch cries were associated with faster heart rate. We also conducted a study with a small rodent, the prairie vole, in my wife's laboratory. My wife is Sue Carter, and Sue is the scientist who discovered the role that oxytocin plays in social bonding. We measured vole heart rate during their vocalizations. We found a similar relation with vole heart rate being correlated with the acoustic features of their vocalizations (Stewart et al., 2015).

In both studies, vocalizations were a reflection of the vagal regulation of their heart—both the infants and the voles were communicating to another conspecific how they "felt." These are examples of what we do in our interactions. We use prosody in our voice to communicate to the biology of the individual—not to their cognitions—whether we are distressed and reactive or calm and safe to come close to.

Let's look at this in terms of social relationships or when we meet people. We might say, "He has good credentials, he seems bright, I agree with his points, but, you know, I just don't trust him." This caution in accepting the person is based on the features cueing our nervous system that the individual is not physically safe to be with.

One of the important evolutionary products embedded in our nervous system is that our nervous system is primed to listen for prosody as a cue to down-regulate our defensiveness. That process of down-regulating defense is coming through this new myelinated vagus.

THE VAGUS AND CARDIOPULMONARY FUNCTION

Dr. Buczynski: Now, you have a lot of thoughts on cardiopulmonary function and the vagus. Can we tie that all together?

Dr. Porges: The simplest take-home point is that our cardiopulmonary system has a job to oxygenate our blood. Oxygen is important to the survival of all mammals including humans. Without sufficient oxygen, we die. The vagus plays an important role in getting oxygen into our blood. The vagus facilitates the diffusion of oxygen into the blood by rhythmically modulating the blood flow and the resistance of the bronchi.

When we start seeing a cluster of disorders within the same person—such as hypertension, sleep apnea, and diabetes—it usually reflects a dysfunction in the myelinated vagus.

There are always psychiatric or psychological correlates to many of these disorders, because the system regulating physiology involving the myelinated vagus is also greatly impacted by the social cues of the environment. The critical point is that the neural circuit regulating social interaction and social engagement behaviors is the same neural circuit that supports health, growth, and restoration.

It's not two disorders, or two diseases, or two disciplines. It's not an internal medicine on one side and a psychology and psychiatry on another side—it's an integrated physiology that is not only regulating health, growth, and restoration but also fostering and supporting social interaction to create safety for the individual.

We haven't used the word safety in this interview yet, but safety is the critical feature here. If our nervous system detects safety, then it's no longer defensive. When it's no longer defensive, then the circuits of the autonomic nervous system support health, growth, and restoration. It's a hierarchy, and the most important thing to our nervous system is that we are safe. When we're safe, magical things occur. They occur on multiple levels, not merely in terms of social relations, but also in accessibility of certain areas of the brain, certain areas of feeling pleasure—being expansive, being creative, and being very positive as well.

Dr. Buczynski: What would that mean for your definition of stress?

Dr. Porges: "Stress" is one of those strange words that's become part of our vocabulary, and it's become such a confusing word that we now talk about "good stress" and "bad stress." I don't even like to use the word! To me, when we use the word "stress," what we're really talking about is mobilization—and mobilization isn't always bad.

Mobilization is part of being a mammal, part of being a human. So the issue is when mobilization doesn't have a functional outcome; then maybe that could be called "maladaptive mobilization," and maybe that's what "stress" is. Here's an example: If you don't like giving interviews or being interviewed and your physiology shifts and your heart starts to beat fast and you want to get out of the situation, but you are unable to get out, your physiology would be supporting mobilization but you can't mobilize—and that would be maladaptive.

THE SIXTH SENSE AND INTEROCEPTION

An interest in our own bodily feelings has been neglected and often disrespected in our contemporary society. Often we have been taught, as part of a strategy to manage our behavior, to reject the feedback that our body is telling us.

If we think about developmental processes within a highly structured socialized environment, we're always telling ourselves not to respond to our bodily needs. We tell ourselves to sit still longer, although we want to get up and move. We also try and delay going to the bathroom when we have urges and not to eat when we get hungry. When we reject these urges and feelings, we are turning off or at least attempting to dampen the sensory component of a feedback loop attempting to regulate physiological processes.

Interoception reflects the feedback from our viscera to our brain. When we understand interoception, we understand that feedback from different physiological states promotes access to different areas of the brain and influences decision-making, memory retrieval, and other cognitive processes.

Dr. Buczynski: Does that relate to higher-level processes?

Dr. Porges: Yes, in a way it does. If you have severe gastric pain, can you function well on high-level cognitive tasks? In the case of gastric pain, the feedback from our viscera limits our ability to think and solve complex problems. Our culture really doesn't have a place for that, so it tries to deal with this by suggesting, "If you feel pain, take medication so you don't feel the pain." But what if pain is your body's attempt to help you or to inform you?

In my world, interoception blends into another construct that I frequently use, which I call neuroception. Neuroception is the nervous system's evaluation of risk in the environment without conscious awareness. When neuroception occurs, we try to generate a narrative to explain why we have the feelings that were triggered. Interestingly, although we are not aware of the cues that trigger neuroception, we are frequently aware, via interoception, of the physiological reactions that were elicited by neuroception.

Neuroception can be illustrated in the following example: You meet someone; the person appears to be bright and physically attractive, but you are not attracted to the person because the person's voice lacks prosody and their facial affect is flat. You don't understand why, but through the process of neuroception, your body has responded, "This is a predator or a person who is not safe," so you develop a personal narrative to make it fit.

HOW VAGAL TONE RELATES TO EMOTION

Let's define the commonly used construct of vagal tone, or more accurately cardiac vagal tone. Vagal tone is used in the literature as a construct reflecting the function of myelinated vagal pathways on the heart. This construct is frequently measured by quantifying the amplitude of an oscillation in the beat-to-beat heart rate pattern that occurs at a periodicity similar to spontaneous breathing. This periodicity in the heart rate is known as respiratory sinus arrhythmia. The profound influence of respiration in dampening vagal influences to the heart during inspiration and enhancing vagal influences to the heart during exhalation provides the physiological basis for this metric. Other estimates of vagal tone have been used based on more global descriptive statistics of heart rate variability.

Now, to relate vagal tone to the regulation of emotion. "Emotion" is a complicated and often ambiguous term, because it deals with a variety of expressions and feelings that are being regulated by different systems. Emotions represent a cluster of psychological constructs. All emotions are not manifestations of the same physiological pathways.

Vocalizations, an important part of emotional expression, are linked to the new mammalian myelinated vagus, because vocalizations and facial expressivity are regulated by an area in the brainstem that regulates the vagus. In fact, myelinated vagal pathways are directly involved in regulating prosodic features of vocalizations.

If you lose control of the myelinated vagus, then the types of emotions you can express change—you lose muscle tone to the upper part of the face, while the muscle tone to the lower part of the face may actually increase. This occurs because the upper part of the face provides major cues of safety, while the lower part of the face is involved in biting and part of the defense system associated with fight/flight behaviors.

Vagal activity and emotions are linked, but there's a second dimension to emotion. The first dimension, which I was talking about, is the common link between the regulation of the striated muscles in the face and head, the intonation of voice, and the vagal control of the heart. But the second one is more dependent on the sympathetic nervous system and reflects the interplay between movement and physiological state. If people are in states of mobilization, the range of emotion that they can express is greatly reduced. If they mobilize, they have to down-regulate the influence of myelinated vagal pathways, and this is manifested in a reduction of vagal tone to the heart.

As an example: Visualize a couple, two people, interacting on treadmills where they're running and moving very rapidly. Their physiological state will shift toward a greater involvement of the sympathetic nervous system as they run. In this mobilized state, you'll see that the range of emotional expressivity becomes limited and their thresholds to be reactive are lowered. Of course, intuitively, you know that this occurs because the physiology during running cannot support the regulation of facial expressions and prosodic vocalizations.

Dr. Buczynski: If vagal regulation is a key part of emotional regulation, then interference with the process would lead to affective disorders.

Dr. Porges: Or misinterpretations of intentions. We could block the expression. If we use Botox on the muscles in the upper face, it will dampen expressions of exuberance. Exuberance and happiness are expressed in the orbicularis oculi, the orbital muscles around the eyes. We look at the upper part of the face for the cues of affect. If we block that, then we may misinterpret their emotional responses. If we block their vagal control of the heart, since the area of the brainstem regulating the vagus is also regulating the face, then they're going to have problems in social interactions.

If the person is taking medications, we have other problems. Many medications have anticholinergic effects, meaning that the medicine blocks cholinergic pathways. The vagus is a major peripheral cholinergic pathway, and thus the medications may change physiological state and the range of emotional expression.

THE VAGAL BRAKE

The "vagal brake" is the reason you can sit there and I can sit here without feeling like we're jumping out of our skin. The vagal brake slows heart rate and is regulated by the myelinated vagus. The vagal brake explains one of the functions of the myelinated vagus as it impacts on the heart's pacemaker, the sinoatrial node.

We often forget that without the vagus, our heart would be beating 20 or 30 beats per minute faster. Without the vagal brake inhibiting the heart's pacemaker, we would have a heart rate over 90 beats per minute. This "braking" of heart rate occurs because the intrinsic rate of the sinoatrial node, the heart's natural pacemaker, is much faster than our normal heart rate.

The vagus provides the "brake" inhibiting the pacemaker slowing our heart rate. This phenomenon provides several important adaptive options. It means that if we want to get our heart rate up 10 beats per minute or 20 beats per minute, we just pull the brake off. We don't need to stimulate the sympathetic nervous system. If we stimulate the sympathetic nervous system, it's a sloppier system—more diffuse—and we may get into states of rage or panic. A mammal has this wonderful ability to increase cardiac output to facilitate mobilization without triggering the sympathetic nervous system. Just by pulling the brake off, we can make these minor adjustments.

HOW NEUROCEPTION WORKS: FEELING THREATENED OR FEELING SAFE

Our nervous system evolved to detect certain features in the environment. Whether they're acoustic features or proximal features of gesture, our nervous system is instantaneously interpreting these features. Much of this interpretation is not on the level of cognitive awareness, so the word "perception" doesn't fit well. So I coined the term "neuroception," which basically means that the nervous system is evaluating risk without requiring a conscious awareness of the risk, and when it evaluates risk, it tries to negotiate, or navigate, or trigger a neural component that fits the context.

If you hear or you're near a person who is engaging, smiling, articulating, and using prosody in voice—the intonation of voice—you may feel very comfortable and want to be close to the person. You'll realize that background sounds disappear; you become interested, your bodily state becomes calm—that's neuroception of safety being triggered by the other person's social engagement system.

In contrast, if you engage a person and they speak with very short phrases and their voice is not prosodic, suddenly your nervous system reacts to that and your body wants to distance itself from the person, because they're now conveying cues to you that they're not safe. These are examples of neuroception.

Some men have this problem—they talk loudly, with a low-frequency voice, and most people, especially women and children, just don't want to be near them. The nervous system, through the process of neuroception, is making this interpretation without you being aware.

Dr. Buczynski: Is neuroception the physiological part of our intuition?

Dr. Porges: I would agree with your interpretation. Neuroception results in a physiological response to features of risk. However, there is a second step. We are often aware of our physiological responses, although we may not be aware of the features in the environment that trigger neuroception. These physiological feelings often influence our personal narrative of the experience. Our story has to fit, and sometimes it's totally irrational: "I like this person/I don't like this person/This person treats me poorly/I don't like going to shopping malls . . ." The person is trying to make their narrative appear to be rational—trying to take this chaotic reaction that doesn't seem to make any sense and make it logical to them.

Dr. Buczynski: We get into that a lot when we're treating trauma and really when we're treating all kinds of conditions, and even in our interpersonal relationships.

Dr. Porges: Yes. We need to realize is that when people get triggered into either mobilization defenses or shutting down, they are going to develop elaborate narratives to make sense of what their body is doing. It is important to acknowledge the awareness of body reactions and that these reactions not only shift physiological state, but also bias perception of the world. Knowledge that physiological state influences our perception of others can be helpful in enabling clients to revise their personal narratives.

Assume you have a stomachache and you're in gastric distress and experiencing severe abdominal pain. How are you going to be with other people? Are you going to be supportive, engaging? Or are you going to be reactive and cranky?

If you have a stomachache, you're not really going to function well at social events. But what if you are unaware that your nervous system is being triggered by context—it's not a gastric distention, but it's something else. Suddenly you feel extraordinarily irritable. Do you want to blame others? Or do you want to try to navigate to a place of safety in this complex world?

I often like to say that when our nervous system fails us, we use behavior. When our nervous system is detecting a neuroception of danger, risk, or fear, maybe we're smart enough to navigate out of it as opposed to beating ourselves up and saying, "You have to stay in that environment."

If we're smart and informed, we listen to our body. If we don't, our nervous system will fail us by not self-soothing and we "act out." In fact, that becomes the term—like the child going into a temper tantrum, we "act out." This inability to down-regulate defense in social contexts functionally reflects that our nervous system has failed us and we "act out." But a more mature person—at least we hope—is informed by an understanding of these systems and can think and navigate and move the body into a less demanding situation.

Most people respond to having a friend in close proximity as making them feel safer. However, if a stranger, who is not a friend, comes into a similar context, their nervous system may go into another state and tell them, "I have to get out of here. I don't trust the person. I'm not safe."

NEUROCEPTION: REACTIONS TO THREAT AND SAFETY

Dr. Buczynski: You've also hypothesized that patients with another construct—borderline personality disorder—might have difficulty maintaining their "vagal brake."

Dr. Porges: Yes, and this goes back to neuroception and what our body detects in evaluating risk in the environment. Borderline individuals may have a neuroception strategy that's very conservative—and let me give you an analogy for that possibility.

When we travel by airplane, we go to the airport where we go through security and are interrogated by the TSA agents. Functionally, a borderline person's nervous system is operating as if they have their own personal TSA agent that is screening others to determine risk. Similar to the TSA agent, their nervous system is saying: "Come on board or don't come on board." If the TSA agent wanted to be a hundred percent sure that there would be no terrorist on the airplane, no one would get on the airplane. In this analogy, the airplane is the borderline person's body and the TSA agent is neuroception. Thus, similar to a TSA agent ensuring that there is no terrorist on the airplane, the borderline's nervous system does not allow another person to be trusted. The risk is so great to certain individuals that they would not allow anyone to get close to them.

Now, let's speculate that the borderline personality's neuroception is set at a threshold that is extraordinarily low and informs them that "If anyone has any feature, they're not coming close to me; I'm going to react to them and I'm going to get away from them." The issue is really that the cues in the environment—the cues of the individual to the borderline trigger defensiveness, when in most other people they wouldn't.

Dr. Buczynski: Where would that lead us, if we follow up that idea?

Dr. Porges: First, let's assume we go no further than understand it; we don't develop any interventions other than having an understanding. If we understood this and informed patients and therapists of these features, that in itself could change how the person reacts. Once they understand what they're doing, there are certain changes due to top-down regulation.

Let me shift the discussion for a moment and talk more about trauma. Then we'll return to borderline. I frequently give talks to groups of therapists who deal with traumatized individuals. I started to convey a theme that focused on understanding and acknowledging that when our body goes into certain states related to being traumatized, it is acting heroically. The body is helping us, it is saving us, and our body is not failing us—it's attempting to help us survive.

The problem is that when our body reflexively puts us into a survival-related state, such as shutting down, we have difficulties navigating out of this state into a state of safety that fosters social engagement. It is important to understand that our bodily reactions that functionally shifted our physiological state were not voluntary. And, when we go into a shutdown state reflexively, the range of voluntary behaviors that we have available is greatly reduced. Our body has changed; it is different. Our body now supports self-protective and not social engagement behaviors.

I encourage therapists to talk to their clients about all the wonderful things that their body did to enable them to survive. Clients need to understand that surviving was the important thing—they survived horrible experiences—and now they need to treat themselves as if they were heroines and heroes.

Therapists have used this information in their practices. They talk to their clients, and the feedback that I get, often through emails, confirms the positive influence of this strategy. Clients have conveyed statements like, "When I could understand this, when my own personal narrative was no longer about blaming my body for not being able to be social but feeling good about what my body did for me, suddenly things became better."

Several therapies employ exposure treatments to desensitize the individual to the trauma stimuli. This behavioral perspective misunderstands the role of physiological state and the defensive state of the client. These procedures, due to the physiological state of the client, rather than dampening reactivity, may increase sensitivity to the stimuli associated with a traumatic event. Instead of confronting the defense systems with cues of trauma, we need to down-regulate the defense systems through top-down influences. We need to use an understanding and respect of the body to down-regulate defenses. Rather than recruiting defenses, we need to understand that our body has done wonderful things for us and we are proud of it and not embarrassed. Then, through these top-down influences embedded in a new personal narrative, a transformation may occur. This strategy is consistent with therapeutic strategies that encourage self-compassion.

I think that something similar might occur with borderline, if we see as a feature of borderline a low threshold to respond defensively to humans. Of course, if you look at the clinical history of a borderline, we frequently see very unpleasant histories. Often within these clinical histories, we see a continuity between earlier trauma experiences and a borderline diagnosis. Perhaps the trauma and abuse history triggered their nervous system into a state in which it was functionally more adaptive for their nervous system to act like a TSA agent who says, "No one is getting on this airplane," and they survive. Now they can understand the adaptive defensive function of these responses. They can be proud of surviving, and they can see the limitations without being angry and disappointed in themselves.

Dr. Buczynski: That reminds me a little bit of the compassion research going on and people studying compassion, self-compassion, and finding that that has a huge impact on behavior change and on depression and anxiety. I'm thinking that your explanation will have a great way of increasing self-compassion, which maybe puts the brain in a totally other state.

Dr. Porges: Yes—and what we're really talking about is putting the nervous system including the brain into a state of safety. Actually, we can flip this a little bit, because when people talk about compassion, they're also often talking about mindfulness, and embedded in mindfulness is being in a state of safety. Mindfulness involves being in a state that is not evaluative or judgmental. As long as we are in that state of safety, it is difficult to recruit our defense systems.

When people are defensive—feeling bad about themselves, feeling angry at someone else—they are recruiting older neural structures. There is an overlap between defensive responses and responses to evaluation. Whenever we are evaluated, we are already recruiting the physiology of defense. Perhaps at the core of borderline personality disorder is a sense of being chronically evaluated that promotes a neuroception of danger. These feelings of danger would produce a chronic state of defense that would negatively bias perception of others.

NOVEL EVENTS: CONTRASTING MAMMALIAN AND REPTILIAN RESPONSES

Dr. Buczynski: Now, I'd like to talk about novel events. You've said that there is a key difference between a mammalian and a reptilian response to novel events. Mammals will direct their attention toward it and communicate about it, whereas with the reptilian response, not so much.

Dr. Porges: Mammalian organisms love novelty, but novelty within a safe environment. Just think about puppies or kittens, or even rat pups—you watch them, and they'll play; there's a novelty, and there's a movement that is away from the mother. But also, if there's something dangerous or fearful, they come back to the mother.

It may appear paradoxical, because those who are bold and seek novelty may also be those who have or who have had the most efficient pathways back to safety. It's not that we seek novelty just for the sake of "seeking novelty." In life, the people who are bold thinkers are willing to take gambles. They're not insecure in novel situations. They're also people who have strong social support networks and don't feel that the gamble is really a life threat.

We can create environmental structures or social structures that support an idealized mammalian model versus a reptilian model. A mammalian model will be empowering of others, more of a shared environment, and have more empathy and care for others. A reptilian model is going to create isolation. It's not going to foster boldness.

Dr. Buczynski: That makes a lot of sense to me except in one kind of case, which would be a type of person who over-seeks novelty—craves or needs a constant danger.

Dr. Porges: Yes, as I was speaking, I was thinking about that as well. As we create a model that results in more optimal behaviors in many individuals, we also see that at the extreme, we start describing sociopathic or some other forms of atypical behavior. The part that I would say is different or may be different is that the healthier behavior involves interactions with others as well.

When one is seeking novelty in bungee-jumping, there is a difference between bungee-jumping with a friend—looking at their face while you're going down at the same time, or skydiving in the arms of another person—versus experiencing an endless series of isolated events that continually trigger the nervous system to mobilize and to stay out of states of immobilization.

Dr. Buczynski: So, that aside, those who are bold and seek novelty are the ones who have the most efficient path back to safety.

Dr. Porges: If we think about the consequences of trauma, it is that traumatized individuals do not seek novelty and don't have a path to safety.

PLAY AS A NEURAL EXERCISE

Let me shift the discussion to play, because I think several clues about the consequences of trauma may come from a better understanding of play. Play recruits the aspects of what might be viewed as defensive systems with social engagement systems: We mobilize, and yet we don't hurt each other. We see the unique role of face-to-face interaction as a defining feature of play in mammals. When mammals play, they continuously present cues of safety and trust through facial expression, and when they cannot maintain face-to-face contact, they're using vocalization cues. They convey to the other that the other is safe to be with. We see this with several species of mammals.

If children don't use face-to-face engagements while playing, then there may be a higher risk of injury. We see this on a playground, where there are children with whom no one wants to play—frequently these children have state regulation problems. They mobilize, when others socially engage, and miss critical cues of social interaction. Often, these mobilization strategies may result in injuries to classmates who are not quick enough to get out of the way. These children don't have an intention to hurt others—they're just unaware of others and do not read other children's social engagement cues.

The route back to more optimal mental health may be through aspects of play. Play involves both mobilization and the inhibition of mobilization. Consistent with the hierarchy described in the Polyvagal Theory, the social engagement system can efficiently inhibit mobilization.

When I was a student, the adaptive function of play was considered to be exercising fight/flight skills. This is what we were taught as an explanation of the play behaviors of young small mammals such as kittens. We can recast this interpretation by understanding the hierarchy of autonomic states as described in the Polyvagal Theory. With this perspective, the primary adaptive function of play behaviors may not be related to the development of hunting or fighting skills but to developing state regulation skills. Play is functionally a neural exercise that enables the playful mammal to move, without fear, through the three polyvagal states: social engagement, mobilization, and immobilization. This neural exercise facilitates transitions among physiological states that would promote resilience and enable the mammal to immobilize without fear while in close proximity to others.

If you watch kittens and puppies, they're always maintaining face-to-face contact when they're playing. They're sufficiently safe with the littermate with whom they are playing to fall sleep without being vigilant. The setting for play is not dangerous. Functionally, they're using the face-to-face interactions of the social engagement system to contain mobilization. Deconstructing this into Polyvagal terms, they are using the myelinated vagus to down-regulate and contain sympathetic nervous system activation.

Our culture confuses play with electronic games, which do not require mobilization, and it confuses solitary exercise with social play. Exercise is primarily without face-to-face, mimicking the physiological state that supports fight/flight behaviors without the resource of the social engagement system.

Dr. Buczynski: If vagal tone is responsible for regulating the body during intense periods of stress, is it possible that the vagus could actually harm the body, especially during a traumatic experience or disruptive event?

Dr. Porges: "Harm" is a complicated construct. Again, one of the features that I tried to embed within the Polyvagal Theory is that physiological responses are not good or bad but have an adaptive consequence.

Then we have to figure out whether those adaptive responses fit the context or don't fit the context—and this removes what I call the "moral veneer" of labeling responses as good or bad, especially when the responses are primarily driven by state shifts in our autonomic nervous system.

It is often assumed that if someone's nervous system is no

longer social after trauma, then something is wrong with them. Instead, they could think of the changes in their nervous system as an adaptive and often a miraculous strategy that their body has implemented to save them injury, death, or pain.

The issue of being injured by the vagus is interesting, because when the subdiaphragmatic vagus is recruited in defense, there can be disruptions in the physiological function of organs below the diaphragm. Specifically, this is often manifested in problems in digestion. Other symptoms may occur that result in the individual going to an internist for diagnoses and treatments.

Individuals, who have experienced trauma, may be greatly affected by this older vagal defense system. If you start looking at the clinical symptomatology of people with trauma histories, we see a lot of subdiaphragmatic issues, whether it's obesity or digestive issues or other types of neurophysiological problems.

Dr. Buczynski: Let's go through that again. Exactly how are you saying that the vagus might be involved?

Dr. Porges: The point missing in our conceptualization of the vagus was that the evolutionarily older unmyelinated vagus that goes predominantly to organs below the diaphragm can respond as a defensive system.

You can readily understand the survival impact of immobilization behaviors, such as passing out and dissociating. But you might not have thought about the health consequences of the recruitment of this system. When there is immobilization in defense and behavior shuts down, the outflow of the subdiaphragmatic vagus may disrupt homeostasis and either surge or become quiescent. This would lead to a cascade of medical problems manifested in the organs located below the diaphragm. Let me put it this way: The neural regulation of the old subdiaphragmatic vagus could be involved in several physical health symptoms that are frequently comorbid with trauma, such as irritable bowel syndrome, fibromyalgia, obesity, and other gut issues.

If we go back to the 1950s, when people had certain types of gastric problems, surgeons performed vagotomies. A vagotomy is a surgical procedure in which the surgeon cuts the subdiaphragmatic branch of the vagus. Since the subdiaphragmatic branch of the vagus was related to release and regulation of acid secretions in the gut, the vagotomy was a medical solution to manage peptic ulcer disease. Vagotomies are no longer common procedures.

Dr. Buczynski: When they would cut it, what was the result for the person?

Dr. Porges: The surgery really wasn't that effective in terms of taking care of the clinical symptoms, and no one, as far as I know, ever studied the consequences of disrupting the neural feedback from the gut to the brain on psychological or physiological domains.

The surgeons were not cutting only the motor pathways; they were also cutting the sensory components of the branch. And they were also influencing other organs that were receiving neural input from the subdiaphragmatic vagus.

But remember, the medical model is, "I have a target organ. If the target organ is dysfunctional, fix the target organ. If the target organ is overresponsive, block the neural influence on that target organ. Do that with medication." But previously they thought about doing it with surgery. A more enlightened strategy would be to understand the neural feedback of these systems and to monitor the responses that they're having on adaptive function.

Dr. Buczynski: Sure. While drugs might be somewhat more enlightened than cutting the vagal nerve, the real way to think about it is to think more about what the function is.

Dr. Porges: Yes. After describing my panic reaction in the MRI (see Chapter 2), I understand that the acute use of drugs may have a very important role in enabling people to function in select contexts when a component of the nervous system is dysfunctional or down-regulated.

Dr. Buczynski: But that's in a situation where you only have to have an MRI once every so often. If you were talking about going on an elevator and you worked on the 25th floor and every day you had to medicate to go to work . . .

Dr. Porges: You're describing the important difference between acute and chronic use of medication. While we know more about the acute use of drugs than the chronic use, a large portion of our society has generalized the positive applications of acute use of drugs to chronic use. For example, there are people taking beta blockers to deal with anxiety issues, public speaking, or perhaps riding an elevator. Beta blockers block a portion of the sympathetic nervous system and remove this adaptive defense option that supports mobilization and hypervigilance. However, since anxiety is also a product of the same neural state that promotes mobilization and hypervigilance, the beta blockers are enablers of people to have experiences that would have triggered a state of defense associated with activation of the sympathetic nervous system.

Most people are prescribed these pharmaceutical aids without considering that they may be blocking the function of an important adaptive component of their nervous system. Once we take a beta blocker, we're blocking a portion of our sympathetic nervous system. What are the long-term effects on health and behavior from this commonly use treatment?

THE VAGUS AND DISSOCIATION

Dr. Buczynski: You had said earlier that you wanted us to get into the vagus and dissociative styles.

Dr. Porges: This is a new area of inquiry for me. We're all students, trying to explore new areas and trying to understand important issues. I hadn't realized how prevalent dissociative states were in people. I didn't understand the process, especially in those who were traumatized.

I'm starting to conceptualize dissociative processes on several levels. At one level, there is the traumatic trigger of an initial dissociation and its link to a phylogenetically old adaptive reaction. Basically, the old vagal circuit enables a biobehavioral shutdown.

When you shut down, heart rate slows. Although this reaction works well in reptiles, it is more challenging to mammals, who have a great need to maintain oxygenated blood to their brains. When mammals shut down, there is a massive reduction in oxygenated blood going to the brain. This compromises function and can result in loss of consciousness.

What happens to our cognitive function when this occurs? Even if the shutdown is not sufficient to result in a loss of consciousness, it changes our awareness, and there is a massive reduction in cognitive resources. The ability to make decisions and even the ability to evaluate the situation may be compromised. These features are consistent with dissociation.

Now, the question is, after this traumatic triggering event, what is the residual effect on our nervous system? Following the traumatic event, is the nervous system more likely to move into a dissociative state? Is there a change in the threshold for becoming dissociative? Then, of course, the real question for trauma survivors and clinicians is: How do we get out of the tendency to dissociate?

The models that we've used have been extraordinarily limited. Historically, the models that have been used for treatment with trauma have been behavioral models—desensitization, visualization, and cognitive behavioral therapy models. But what we haven't used or thought about is a model that is very similar to taste aversion—a one-trial conditioning model in which, with a single exposure, something gets associated and triggers us and puts us into a specific physiological state.

We have to think that taste aversion is also dependent on the subdiaphragmatic vagus, the older unmyelinated vagal pathway and not the mammalian myelinated supradiaphragmatic vagal pathway. Taste aversion produces a regurgitative response that has adaptive function following the ingestion of contaminated foods. Taste aversion, similar to immobilization and dissociation, attempts to minimize life threat and internal injury.

I'm trying to figure out now if the science of the 1940s and 1950s studying the concept of single-trial learning will provide insight into the process through which one traumatic incident changes behavior and the changed behavior is very resistant to modification. Taste aversion is an example of single trial learning, which links an event with a subdiaphragmatic vagal reaction.

I will be investigating what was learned in the animal research on single-trial learning, especially with taste aversion paradigms. I want to learn the methods that were used to reverse the effect and how successful they were. From that literature, we might find clues to move trauma survivors toward more adaptive social behavior. The clues are going to be embedded in an understanding that several features of trauma are products of the subdiaphragmatic vagus adaptively reacting in defense.

Where in the nervous system is the memory of this single-trial link between traumatic event and subdiaphragmatic response stored? What does our nervous system do with these stored memories? These questions have not been answered.

Dr. Buczynski: Stephen, how did you get into thinking about that?

Dr. Porges: The features are all about immobilization, and I think it's just like the vagal paradox. It's about using certain words—whether we use words like "vagus" or "behavior," if we don't deconstruct them, we're very limited in what we can understand. When we start to deconstruct the words into dynamic regulatory processes, we start seeing that the components become understandable.

Let's think about certain types of learning. Those of us who went to graduate school in the late 1960s dealt with the expectation that the theoretical models for psychology would be behavioral models and that these models could be applied to bodily processes in order to gain control over visceral organs. These would be the same models that were used to control the behavior of fingers, hands, and limbs.

In the late 1960s and early 1970s, scientists made a grave mistake, because they were treating the neural regulation of visceral organs as if they were following the same rules that explained the learned modifications of conscious operant behaviors. Once they started to realize that they were different and followed different "rules," they lost interest in understanding how to directly control visceral organs.

Biofeedback is a discipline that tries to improve health by applying learning and conditioning principles to modify the neural regulation of the heart or other organs. However, no longer do biofeedback researchers think that they directly influence the neural pathways regulating the autonomic nervous system. They no longer even talk that way. They describe the outcome of their treatments as improving health and function without attributing a direct causal pathway.

In early research on biofeedback and operant conditioning of physiological activity, researchers were attempting to explain how to control the visceral organs, composed of smooth and cardiac muscle, without the involvement of skeletal muscle. Voluntary movements use skeletal muscles, which indirectly influence autonomic state. A big scientific question in the early 1970s was whether operant learning principles could influence the heart without the involvement of skeletal muscles. Could the brain directly control the heart through a learning paradigm? Although scientists initially published promising results, their results could not be replicated. The reliability of these negative results confirmed an earlier view that organs of the autonomic nervous system could not be controlled through the operant learning strategies that were effective in conditioning the behaviors dependent on skeletal muscles. Unfortunately, lost was a quest to understand the laws of learning that could influence the regulation of visceral organs.

The scientific background investigating the involuntary

nature of visceral responses is critical to our understanding of the effects of trauma and how we explain how a single traumatic event can functionally "retune" the autonomic nervous system. Trauma provides a profound example of adaptive reactions, which gets clouded when we start discussing PTSD and other checklist defined clinical diagnoses. Some individuals with a diagnosis of PTSD have never experienced a shutdown response, while others without a diagnosis have. These observations indicate that some reactions to traumatic events are highly mobilized, defensive, highly anxious reactive behaviors, while other reactions are manifested totally in immobilization.

To clarify the diagnosis, I think we need to understand the mechanisms mediating these different reactions. We need to emphasize that the dagnosis should not be based on the events, but on the reactions to the events.

Dr. Buczynski: What might that look like?

Dr. Porges: From my perspective, I'd like to look at a subcategory—immobilized and dissociated or passed out in response to the trauma—versus others.

Dr. Buczynski: You talked about a single-trial approach.

Dr. Porges: Yes, that would be a single event that triggered trauma versus an accumulation of numerous events. I think the mechanisms underlying a trauma reaction to a single event are different than the accumulated effects of repeated abuses that define complex trauma. From a scientific perspective, it is easier to study the mechanisms of a single-event trauma and potentially to create an animal model that will provide insights into understanding and treating trauma in humans.

The single-event model would lead us to ask clients different questions. I think we need very detailed clinical histories—we need to get the individual to describe their response and their feeling more than we need descriptions of the event. If we get more information about their personal experiences, behaviors, and feelings—whether they passed out, whether they dissociated, whether they fantasized, what happened during the abuse and what happened after the event, that's the critical point. Then we can start working on an intervention model that will move the nervous system out of states of defense.

My own strategy, or at least my initial one—and it may not be correct—is that as long as you have features of the social engagement system on board through the use of modulated prosodic voice or safe environments, then you might be able to get the person out of that defensive immobilization state. Our social engagement system with the myelinated vagus—our face, our voice, our ability to utilize prosodic features, and our ability to listen to prosodic voices—enables us to change our physiological state and the physiological state of others. Functionally, the social engagement system provides portals for intervention and treatment.

If we can change the physiological state to be incompatible with shutting down, then I think we can move the person out of it. The most successful trauma therapists are those that enable their clients to negotiate and navigate in a state of safety. By navigating or negotiating with the client's safety, the person is no longer dependent on their defensive systems to shut down or to mobilize.

SINGLE-TRIAL LEARNING

Dr. Buczynski: When you talk about single-trial learning, tell us more about what you think that might look like.

Dr. Porges: The most frequently used example of single-trial learning is the link between chemotherapy or radiation and taste aversion. When patients receive chemotherapy or radiation treatments, the food they ate before the therapy becomes sufficiently aversive to trigger nausea long after they have the therapy. Note that the unmyelinated vagus is involved in nausea.

The question now is what are the strategies that scientists have used to get people out of those reactions?

I would basically say that in the single-trial trauma reaction of shutting down, the person is normal or typical before this event, and after the event, the person can't be in public places, starts having lower-gut issues, can't deal with proximity of others, is hypersensitive to low-frequency sounds, and even may have symptoms of fibromyalgia and unstable blood pressure.

Individuals with these symptoms provide a window to understand underlying mechanisms. We get hints about the mechanism, because several symptoms are mediated through the old unmyelinated subdiaphragmatic vagus. These features reflect a massive vagal reaction characteristic of the unmyelinated vagus being recruited in defense.

I am proposing that if the old vagus is recruited in defense in response to a trauma event, it is functionally manifested as an example of single-trial learning. Once the unmyelinated vagus is recruited in defense, the individual's neural regulation is different and reorganized in a way that is resistant to modification and a natural return to former homeostatic state. Thus, reactions to trauma appear to be very similar to the taste aversion model. These speculations, hopefully, will lead to insights into deconstructing the mechanisms of the immobilization reaction to trauma.

Dr. Buczynski: I love the way you're moving in another direction, and I'll be picking up on it as the journey is in process.

Dr. Porges: It is really quite a wonderful journey—and this is what life is about. I mentioned the notion of boldness and good social relationships—you don't go places with your mind unless you have a good place to go with your body.

I'm focusing on these issues, and I'm glad you're picking up on them. I'm really interested in the fact that the world we live in focuses so much on cognitive functioning without an integration of our cognitions with our bodily experiences, and that this leads to a type of dissociation that is occupying a significant percentage of everyone's lives.

5

CUES OF SAFETY, HEALTH, AND POLYVAGAL THEORY

Stephen W. Porges and Ruth Buczynski

THE VAGUS AND POLYVAGAL THEORY

Dr. Buczynski: Let's recap by first talking about the vagus—the primary function of it in the brain and the body.

Dr. Porges: The vagus is the major nerve of the parasympathetic nervous system, and functionally it connects our brain to our body.

In fact, Darwin, in his book on emotions in man and animals, described the vagus—he called it the pneumogastric nerve—a very important nerve connecting the two most important organs of the body: the brain and the heart (Darwin, 1872). The vagus is a nerve that comes off the brain. It is a cranial nerve that goes directly to the heart and to other visceral organs.

The vagus is involved in the regulation of physiological processes involving visceral organs, including the heart and the gut. The bidirectional function of the vagus is an extremely important feature that is frequently neglected. The vagus is not only sending signals from the brain to visceral organs; it is also sending signals from visceral organs to the brain. The vagus is involved in both top-down and bottom-up functions.

Eighty percent of the fibers in the vagus are sensory. Now that we are becoming very interested in brain–body and mind–body relationships, the vagus is a primary neural portal.

Dr. Buczynski: Now, your theory isn't called Vagal Theory—it is called Polyvagal Theory. Tell us about that.

Dr. Porges: First, there is the neurobiology that is very well established, and then there is the theory. The neurobiology includes the fact that in mammals the vagus contains two motor pathways with different functions that evolved at different times during the evolution of vertebrates. This becomes extremely important because the roles they play are very different. The different vagal pathways originate in two different areas of the brainstem. One area (i.e., nucleus ambiguus) is linked with the regulation of all the facial muscles—muscles of ingestion, muscles of listening, and muscles of engaging others. Our social nervous system is intimately related with this evolutionarily newer vagus—and so is our breath.

Dr. Buczynski: That's the newer one?

Dr. Porges: Yes, that's the evolutionarily newer one—meaning it evolved with mammals. We have to remember that mammals are very special vertebrates—they need other mammals to regulate their bodily states and to survive. This becomes part of a theme that we will get into. Trauma disrupts the ability to relate to others and to use social behavior to literally regulate vagal function—to calm us down.

The second vagus goes below our diaphragm—it is subdiaphragmatic—and we share this with other vertebrates like reptiles, even fish. The two vagal circuits work in harmony with the sympathetic nervous system to enable us to optimize physiological processes and health, but they also react to the world—we use them as defenses or responses to social challenges.

Now I am going to take a little segue. Most of us learned about the autonomic nervous system, and we learned that there was a sympathetic nervous system that supported our aggressive drive, such as fight/flight behaviors, and was involved in stress-related responses. We learned that the parasympathetic nervous system with the vagus supported health, growth, and restoration and that the parasympathetic and sympathetic nervous systems were in battle. These generalizations are partially, but not totally true.

We need to think differently about how the components of our autonomic nervous system are recruited to respond to challenges in the world. If we are talking to each other in a safe environment, there is no danger and no reason to stimulate our sympathetic nervous system to support fight or flight behaviors.

Being in a safe environment doesn't mean we should turn off the sympathetic nervous system. We need sympathetic activation, independent of the demands of fight and flight defenses. The sympathetic nervous system is important to us: It helps blood flow and makes us feel alert and confident. However, we don't use the sympathetic nervous system to initiate positive social behavior. If we did, we might shift into a defensive state. If we shift to a defensive sympathetic state, we will bias our neuroception of the intentions of others and interpret them more negatively. In terms of our normal social behavior, we want to use the newer vagus to optimize social engagement behaviors and to contain the autonomic nervous system from shifting into defensive states.

Now we need to discuss the theory part of the Polyvagal Theory. The theory proposes a hierarchy in how these neural circuits react to the world. The theory proposes that, similar to the function of the brain in which evolutionarily newer circuits inhibit older ones, the neural circuits that regulate the visceral organs that evolved earlier are inhibited by the evolutionarily newer circuits (see dissolution).

Based on our knowledge of the evolutionary changes in the autonomic nervous system, the oldest system represented in mammals is the unmyelinated subdiaphragmatic vagus, which when recruited in defense would shut us down—similar to the defensive strategies of many reptiles. Reptiles freeze and immobilize to reduce metabolic activity; they go underwater for several hours without breathing.

The next stage of evolutionary changes in the autonomic nervous system was the emergence of a spinal sympathetic nervous system that supported flight/fight behaviors.

With the evolution of mammals, a new neural circuit evolved that integrated social behavior with the regulation of physiological state. The new vagal system enabled mammals to socially interact with each other. This vagal system basically enabled social behavior to choreograph and functionally protect the other components of the autonomic nervous system to support homeostatic functions.

When the new mammalian vagal system is working well, then subdiaphragmatically, the sympathetic and parasympathetic nervous systems are functioning in a homeostatic dance reflecting the positive features of autonomic balance.

When I talk to clinicians who are dealing with clients who have trauma histories, they report that many of their clients have digestive problems—gastric distress or constipation.

Polyvagal Theory suggests that this dysfunction of the subdiaphragmatic vagal circuit is due the recruitment of this circuit in defense, which disrupts its role in supporting homeostasis.

When people are in states of flight/fight and fear or danger, the neural regulation of the subdiaphragmatic area is depressed. When they are highly mobilized in fight/flight or stress behaviors, sympathetic activation is high, while the function of both branches of the vagus is down-regulated. However, the Polyvagal Theory proposes that in response to life threat, both the supradiaphragmatic vagus and the sympathetic nervous system are down-regulated, enabling the subdiaphragmatic vagus to be recruited in defense. The product of this old defense system is immobilization in an attempt to be inanimate, with reflexive shifts in blood pressure resulting in passing out and a potential surge in dorsal vagal outflow resulting in defecation. Based on the theory, we can see that these different neural circuits support different ranges of behavior for mammals—and of course humans.

HOW THE MIND—BODY CONNECTION IMPACTS MEDICAL CONDITIONS

We live in a medically oriented world that treats organs as if each organ can be treated independently and is not part of an integrative and interactive autonomic nervous system.

We can talk philosophically, but we may need to talk pragmatically. I have been involved in medical education now as a professor in a medical school for the last 15 years. In this role, I learned that physicians are not very informed about the role of the nervous system in terms of regulating the organs that they treat.

When we use the term "nervous system," we already are implicitly describing a system that has connections between the brain and the body. We don't have an autonomic nervous system that is below the neck and a central nervous system that is in the head. We have a nervous system that is reading our body and is changing our brain based upon the feedback it is getting from the body—and of course our brain can down-regulate actions of the body, both observable movements and visceral functions.

We can talk about peripheral symptoms—and remember, we can start categorizing symptoms into supradiaphragmatic—occurring above the diaphragm—and subdiaphragmatic—occurring below the diaphragm. Tightly wrapped people, who are highly anxious, may be expressing symptoms related to the use of the sympathetic nervous system as a defense system. Only when the supradiaphragmatic vagus is suppressed or functionally withdrawn can the sympathetic nervous system be used efficiently in defense. Interestingly, we see clusters of clinical symptoms, such as hypertension and cardiovascular disease and other autonomic disorders of organs above the diaphragm, linked to low supradiaphragmatic vagal tone and an activated sympathetic nervous system.

For survivors of trauma and chronic abuse, the subdiaphragmatic vagal system may have been recruited in defense. This may occur during states of dissociation. When the subdiaphragmatic vagus is used in defense, a different array of clinical disorders may appear. Clients might have fibromyalgia, digestive and bowel problems, and difficulties having and enjoying sex, although they may want to. We see this in women, who may defecate while having sex, because the subdiaphramatic vagus might react in defense.

Several clinical symptoms that are viewed within the medical world as being end-organ-related may be related to a disruption in the neural regulation of these organs. However, few physicians are adequately aware of the contribution of the nervous system to the function of visceral organs. And being aware may lead to better explanations and treatments of the disorder.

Without an organizing principle, such as neural regulation, providing an understanding of the mechanisms leading to clinical disorders, diagnosis may lead to a loss of control and feelings of hopelessness. An important part of Polyvagal Theory is to inform survivors that they're not victims and that their symptoms are a functional product of a neural control system that enabled them to adapt and survive.

TRAUMA AND VIOLATIONS OF TRUST

Dr. Buczynski: You have mentioned the profound impact that trauma frequently has on violations of trust, or feeling safe.

Dr. Porges: If a person has been psychologically injured in a relationship, what is the best way of not getting injured? The best way of not getting injured is not to trust anyone. This is what the social engagement system is about—it is all about giving cues to the other of safety and enabling proximity. The social engagement system triggers neuroception to make the other person comfortable.

If the other person was comfortable at one point and then got injured, the social engagement system is now going to be down-regulated; it is going to be tuned to not allow anyone else to come close emotionally and perhaps physically. People who have been severely hurt emotionally in a relationship find it difficult to create new relationships, even though on a cognitive level creating a relationship may be a very high priority. They may desperately want relationships, but their bodies are saying no.

I try to explain to trauma survivors what their body has done. There seems to be a prevalent implicit feeling for many survivors of trauma that their body has done something wrong, something very bad. They need to be informed that their bodily response strategies may have been protective and saved their lives. Their bodily responses may have enabled them by immobilizing and dissociating to minimize physical injury and painful suffering by not fighting back. The immobilization may be very adaptive, since it may not trigger additional aggression.

There are several adaptive functions of surviving through immobilization or dissociation. The question is: How does your personal narrative explain these immobilization responses? How do you use that information to see who you are? Do you see yourself as victim, or do you see yourself now as heroic?

I received an email from a woman who was in her late sixties, and she described her experiences. When she was a teenager, a person attempted to strangle her and then raped her. Many years later, she was telling this to her daughter, and the daughter asked, "Why didn't you fight? Why didn't you do something?" The mother was embarrassed and felt shame. Then she said, "I read about your Polyvagal Theory, and suddenly I feel vindicated and I'm crying now."

I was crying, too, just reading the email. But the issue was that she understood that her bodily reaction of immobilizing was protective. She realized on a visceral level that she felt proud of her bodily responses. Her bodily reaction was heroic; she was not a victim.

We forget that some bodily reactions are reflexive and not voluntary. Immobilization in response to life threat is a common "reflexive" response shared with several other mammalian species. Our society treats people who don't fight or who don't effectively mobilize as if there is something wrong with them. Instead, a Polyvagal-informed society would be saying, "This really was the best neurobiologically adaptive response that you could've made, and it is fortunate that your body made that decision for you. If you had fought, you might be dead."

This is all about how we interpret our own behaviors—how we develop our personal narrative.

Dr. Buczynski: Yes, and for the mental health folks on the webinar, this gives us a biological explanation of the idea that we've been talking about with patients for years: "You survived in the best way you knew how." Perhaps that can help them feel really understood and, as you said, vindicated. Maybe they can celebrate that or feel respect for the courage they had.

Dr. Porges: Yes, it is all about being informed. If we superimpose that moral veneer when the culture says, "This is bad," then we say, "I guess I was bad." If we remove the moral veneer and understand our neurobiological adaptive reactions, then we start to see the advantages of our reactions.

HOW NEUROCEPTION WORKS

The idea of a neurobiological, adaptive reaction to threatening events has a profound effect on our conceptualization of trauma. Functionally, our nervous system is continuously evaluating risk outside the realm of conscious awareness and reflexively shifts physiological state to optimize categories of behavior—social engagement, fight/flight, or shutdown. In a sense, the nervous system is attempting to move into a physiological state that would support the most adaptive behavior, at least the most adaptive as interpreted by the nervous system. I have called this process "neuroception." Sometimes we are not prepared for these adaptive reactions and the reaction is a surprise—for example, experiencing panic while in a MRI or other confined space, feeling dizzy when reprimanded, or fainting while giving a talk.

We are also vulnerable to faulty neuroception, when the nervous system detects risk when there no risk or when the nervous system detects safety when there is risk.

There are people who pass out during public speaking, and it is not really that they get anxious—they just go *whoosh* and they faint. Fainting, known clinically as vasovagal syncope, is due to a rapid and massive drop in blood pressure, which results in insufficient oxygenated blood flow to the brain. This reaction is often due to the nervous system detecting cues of life threat. Once this neurophysiological response occurs, the conscious brain tries to make sense of the sequence and builds a plausible personal narrative. Often the personal narrative focuses on self-esteem, but the cause of the reaction may not be related to self-esteem; it may be triggered by another feature in their environment, such as confinement or isolation.

For me, I had a panic reaction while having a clinical scan in the restricted space of an MRI (see Chapter 2). I was surprised and shocked that my body went into this defensive state. I don't enjoy confined spaces but didn't think going into an MRI would trigger a state of panic. I am frequently in relatively confined spaces. I fly a lot. I don't like middle seats, although I can tolerate them. But most people don't like them. From my perspective, based on my own knowledge of my bodily reactions over decades, my reaction was totally unanticipated.

Mammals do not like forced confinement. Across mammalian species, the most potent stressors appear to be isolation and restraint. Just think of those two stressors in the world in which we live, and think about it, too, in terms of medicine and what we do to people in our care.

Dr. Buczynski: Yes, and I imagine you've had, through your recent personal experiences, a chance to see that close up.

Dr. Porges: Yes, and I'll share that with you. I was diagnosed last April with prostate cancer, and I didn't have the options of not doing anything—which is what I suggested to physicians, and they didn't appreciate my suggestion. The biopsy showed some fairly aggressive cancerous tissue, so I was given the option of broad-beam radiation or radical prostatectomy.

There are a couple of things involved here. First, I'm fine now. The point I want to make is that when you receive a diagnosis, and even if you're well informed, your body may start to shut down. I was monitoring what happened to me following the diagnosis. I felt it in the legs. Many of the people listening will know what I mean. I was on my way to shutting down, which I knew was not a good thing.

Even though I was informed, there were still the uncertainties of medical diagnosis, and the uncertainties of treatment can be very disruptive. We don't know how our body will respond. Regardless of what we know about the disease, its treatment, and the probabilities of recovery, there will still be uncertainty.

I developed a strategy to deal with this life-threatening diagnosis. The first thing I did was to delay surgery until August. Many people who get diagnoses can't wait to get started with the treatment, even in situations when cancers grow slowly—delaying treatment bothers them too much.

I delayed surgery to August for two reasons: First, I would have had to cancel several trips, and this would have been very hard for me to do. As profoundly disruptive as the diagnosis was, the act of canceling trips bothered me even more. I had to clear my calendar for three months to deal with the surgery and recovery—something I had never done before, but I did it. Second, I wanted to get in physical shape for the surgery to improve my recovery trajectory. I started to exercise, lost about 10 pounds, and improved my physical fitness.

Prior to the surgery, I continued to give talks and workshops. These opportunities to interact provided a vehicle to connect with people. I was using my talks as my own therapy. By the end of my series of talks—I had to give maybe 8 or 10 talks, and that included two European trips—I felt totally connected and wonderful. I was ready for surgery. I felt that if life were to end, it would be okay, because I experienced connectedness. I felt good about my family; I felt good about my life. It was really quite an interesting experience with minimal stress and no feelings of panic. I also listened to guided imagery tapes during the two weeks prior to surgery.

I had the surgery 2 miles from where I live. I could see the hospital from my home office window. I was, in a sense, among friends. As I went to the hospital for surgery, I had wonderful visualizations and positive thoughts.

When I was on the operating table, I talked to the anesthesiologist, and I said to him, "You know, it's your job to keep me alive during this procedure."

Dr. Buczynski: No pressure!

Dr. Porges: Yes, but the scrub nurse said, "No, it's all our jobs to keep you alive." I asked the anesthesiologist what my heart rate was, and it was in the mid-sixties. It was seven-thirty or eight in the morning, and they were going to cut me open. I did not have any preoperative medication. I was totally relaxed. Following the surgery, which lasted for about five hours, I suffered little pain or discomfort except during the first day, which was due to the position of my body during surgery. But I was really fine.

There were two processes going on: First, I was conceptualizing the surgery as being helpful, not hurtful; and second was the loss of any panic or fear of death. These processes contributed to a reconceptualization of my role as a human being. I had learned from this personal journey of giving talks and interacting with people that the true value in life is connectedness with other people. I felt really good . . . so that's my personal story.

Dr. Buczynski: And I'm so glad you're okay. Thank you for sharing—sometimes we define trauma in a limited way. We define it as something that happens in war or in a car crash, or through rape or sexual molestation or being beaten. But there is a lot more trauma than that. In fact, I think it would be important for the folks who are nurses and physicians on the webinar to think about whether that might be something to include in their own thinking in working with a patient who has had, let's say, a myocardial infarction, or who has just had a diagnosis or is going through a procedure—what that might be like for them.

UNCERTAINTY AND THE BIOLOGICAL IMPERATIVE OF CONNECTEDNESS

Dr. Porges: Much of our life experiences is linked to the issue of uncertainty, which is a part of disconnecting from other people. I've started using a term—a new term for me—that is used by others in biology. I'm talking about a biological imperative—what is the primary biological imperative for humans? It is to be connected to other humans.

When we elect to have surgery or any medical procedures, we forget that we are not a machine like a car and that the people administrating the treatment are not the equivalent of automobile repairmen. We are not a car that gets something replaced or repaired—human organs are not equivalent to an automobile part. We are not a machine—we are a dynamically interacting living biological system. When we touch something, we touch everything within us and we also touch the people that we interact with. Physicians in the medical community need to become more connected to people they are treating.

As we are watching, medicine is becoming more manualized; treatments are not very flexible and are not individualized to the patient. This is even occurring in psychiatry. It begins with the medical records—when you go into a physician's office, the physician rotates sideways and looks at the computer monitor and not at the patient. The physician focuses attention on the computer monitor and starts typing as opposed to providing the patient with the reassurance of an engaged face-to-face interaction that respects the patient's need to feel safe.

For me, I felt very grateful for my treatment by the

University of North Carolina medical system. The people were wonderful and engaging. I felt connected to the community. When I lived in Chicago, which has good medical services, I didn't feel invited into a community when receiving medical treatments; treatments were more detached and characterized by an efficient depersonalized "in and out" of the medical facilities.

I still have friends in Chicago, and they are professors, physicians, and businesspeople. When they have medical procedures, they are alone. They may not have met or talked to their physicians or their surgeons prior to their procedures. Being in a smaller community was very nice—it was nice to meet the people who were treating me beforehand.

POLYVAGAL THEORY: TRAUMA AND ATTACHMENT

Dr. Buczynski: Let's stay with this idea of engagement and connection, because I agree—it is so important. Does Polyvagal Theory have anything to say about the relationship between trauma and attachment?

Dr. Porges: Yes it does. If trauma disrupts the ability to feel safe with another, then the underlying roots upon which attachment is based are ruptured. I guess the way to phrase it is like this: If there is a good, underlying developmental base for attachment, then a person has a buffer for trauma.

I don't know if that's been studied, but one starts to see the patterns of life. We see the development of people we've known since childhood, and some of them are no longer with us, but we see patterns in their lives. We see them over a span—50 or 60 years later—and what is remarkable is that some of the strategies are still in place that they used when they were children, whether or not they ever got informed by their behavior, or they were able to remodel or reorganize.

I'm beginning to see and think that what we really need to do is inform ourselves about the disruptive things that may have happened to us—not to be angry or to blame, but to try to understand the strategies that our body has taken to adapt and to survive. Then we can evaluate whether those are really good strategies.

This all folds back into what we could call our own personal narrative, and how we use that narrative either to modify our behaviors to be more compassionate, more loving, more successful human beings, or to be more driven, more tightly wrapped, more aggressive, and more self-oriented. At some point, it becomes our choice—when we are informed, we can develop strategies to make ourselves feel safer.

Dr. Buczynski: But not necessarily by just deciding to feel safer.

Dr. Porges: Your point is extremely important because these are not voluntary decisions to be different, although it is a voluntary decision to try to develop the toolkit or the neural circuits necessary to become more resilient and safer.

Let me play with this idea. Let's assume that we are driven—we are professors writing grants, writing articles, no time to talk to anyone. We have to get the next grant out and we have a heart attack—not surprising!

Then something happens: We start to understand that there is a neural connection between our brain and our body. As we learn more about how the autonomic nervous system regulates our viscera, we realize that we often implement a maladaptive strategy by turning off feedback from our body.

If we think about this, we realize that this is limiting our life experiences. Can we recover? Can we build on some of the neural circuits that will enable us to live a richer life or a more social life? This really does get at notions of trauma treatment or trauma therapy, and the answer is that there are some strategies.

If we look at it from a decontextualized neurobiological perspective, we begin to say, "It would be nice if this newer social engagement system with the myelinated vagus came on board to down-regulate my natural tendency to become combative, defensive, or go into rage. I am beginning to understand that these defensive behaviors serve an adaptive function in keeping me from shutting down, and I have a history of shutting down."

In a sense, we create a whole hierarchy. Let's just say that I had a shutdown experience; I was restrained, I was abused when I was young, and my adaptive behavior is to keep moving because, as long as I keep moving, I can't shut down. But if I keep moving, I can't relate—I can't enjoy, I can't create relationships—and I really want a relationship.

We can understand that there is a biology to turning off or down-regulating this mobilization defense system. It is all about the social engagement system, and it is about the myelinated vagus. We can do some very simple yet very profound exercises, such as breathing. Learning different breathing patterns is helpful, because slow, deep exhalations can calm us down by stimulating vagal inhibition of the sympathetic nervous system. If we vocalize while slowly exhaling, we are singing. What is playing a wind instrument? It is dependent on slowly exhaling. What is talking with long phrases without interrupting? We are vocalizing while slowly exhaling.

We can efficiently shift our physiology through social behavior, through playing music, and even listening to music. These behaviors will, through neural feedback circuits, change the vagal regulation to our heart and influence the entire social engagement system by improving our ability to listen (e.g., via middle ear muscles) and to express positive feelings (e.g., via facial expressions and vocal prosody).

HOW SINGING AND LISTENING CALM US

Dr. Buczynski: I understand how singing is a slow exhalation, but how is listening a slow exhalation?

Dr. Porges: Listening is very special. Listening is a portal to trigger the entire social engagement system.

Remember how you talk to your dog or talk to your child or talk to your friend. If you use a voice with prosodic intonations. These vocal features characterized by modulating tone triggers in the nervous system a neuroception of safety.

A portal to change physiology can be through breath, but it also can be through listening.

We've had some discussions about certain types of music before, but certain types of music do trigger a sense of safety. I remember in a previous webinar we talked about Johnny Mathis (see Chapter 2). Recently, I was watching a documentary video on Harry Nilsson, who had a beautiful tenor voice. He wasn't the safest person, but his voice was really beautiful and melodic, and the songs he wrote also carried and created relaxation. It is because our nervous system evolved to detect those modulations as cues of safety.

When we know the importance of vocalizations as cues of

safety, we can create contexts to enable people to feel safer. This feeling of safety *is* the treatment—it is a neural exercise.

Dr. Buczynski: What you just said is really important: *Feeling safe is the treatment.* That might be a way to organize your thinking—whatever your profession is—whether you are on the mental health side or a physician helping someone who is very sick.

Dr. Porges: It is a powerful concept. I had a slide in one of my talks that said our nervous system interprets or defines safety much differently than the legal or cultural standards do. For example, having a teacher carrying a gun—having a principal walking around with a gun—may be a way of making schools safe from a legal point of view, but it certainly creates a context that the nervous system doesn't like to experience. Our bodies detect features of safety and features of danger, and we need to understand that.

Also, we need to remember that we live in a culture where people say, "It is really *what* I say and not *how* I say it that's important." But our nervous system is telling us something different to us: It says, "It is not really *what* you say—it is *how* you say it."

Dr. Buczynski: Going back to the whole idea of music: How might a practitioner—and in this case, I'm thinking of a mental health practitioner—incorporate music into the treatment of someone who has experienced trauma?

Dr. Porges: We first need to think about what to remove from the acoustic environment before we start talking about what to put into it.

Low-frequency sounds are profound signals to a neuroception of danger and life threat. We don't want our nervous system to be hypervigilant for danger and life threat.

First of all, we want our clinical rooms, our consultation rooms, to be quiet. We don't want them to have low-frequency sounds from elevators, ventilation systems, or traffic. We don't want these rooms near elevators or noisy corridors or break rooms. We want the rooms to be quiet because the nervous system is going to be detecting these low-frequency sounds as if there is impending doom—as if something bad is going to happen.

These clues were known to the composers of the classic symphonies, who relaxed their audiences with the first movement of their symphonies by using lullabies—the voice of violins, the mother's voice. Once the audience felt safe with the introduction of the melody, the composers moved the melody to lower-pitch instruments until the listener felt save with those sounds. In many compositions the first movement is a relaxing safe experiences in which the melody is shared among the full tonal range of the orchestra. However, the experience frequently is very different during the second movement. The second movement is often characterized by acoustic signals of impending doom—monotonic with low frequencies. The classical composers understood the profound impact of acoustic stimulation on bodily state and feelings, which we can measure in our physiology. They created their own scenarios—their own narratives—with the music.

A clinician can be intuitive as well and start removing the low-frequency sounds—which convey impending doom to the client—and then enable the individual to listen to vocals, especially female vocals, to help relax and stimulate the social engagement system.

Acoustic stimulation in certain frequency ranges can be very comforting and calming. Do you remember the music of the sixties? There was folk music, which was, again, extraordinarily prosodic. Pete Seeger, who recently died, was at the vanguard of this movement of singing songs of social change—these were important and serious songs. However, they were put to music that was frolicking and light, and people could sing along. People felt good listening—this was part of the whole tradition of folk music to convey important ideas without scaring people.

Music can be used in the clinical setting. What's most important for the clinician is to get rid of the low-frequency sounds, use prosodic voice, and if a person is gaze-averting or turning away from you, don't force eye contact—they're too scared already. If they're gaze-averting, they're probably scared. When in a fear state, people aren't comfortable with direct eye gaze, although they will spontaneously turn toward you once they feel more comfortable.

Dr. Buczynski: If you are a clinician and you don't have control over those factors—the ventilation in the building, or how close we are to traffic noise—what would you recommend?

Dr. Porges: I would recommend looking for another office. That would be my first choice.

Dr. Buczynski: But you might work for a hospital or . . .

Dr. Porges: I don't think we spend enough time thinking about the physical characteristics of where we are delivering our services. The rooms themselves have therapeutic consequences. If the acoustic stimulation, where we see our patients, is so profound and unambiguous to our nervous system, it is going to interfere with our ability to deliver our services.

Sometimes clinicians will use a white-noise generator in an attempt to mask these sounds—often this is unsuccessful and just ramps up the background information that the nervous system has to process. People in that environment might appear to be hyperaroused, when in a quiet environment they may start to become calm.

I've had several discussions with architects, and I have even talked at some architectural meetings about the notion of designing space for wounded warriors that would be therapeutic and not solely focus on aesthetics. Architects are usually more concerned about appearance, and in medical environments they are concerned about cleanliness and the ability to monitor patients. If you were designing a hospital, you would want to be able to monitor the health of the patients and to ensure that the space was clean. However, I am less interested in the surveillance features and the aesthetic aspects of the space and more interested in how well the space absorbs sound and makes the body feel.

So, to your point about what you can do—most offices have walls and floors constructed of a hard surface. Sound bounces off these surfaces, often resulting in a noisy work environment. These surfaces can be modified by using wall hangings and putting carpets on the floor—and both are sound absorbing and can make a room feel safe and comfortable. These options might be a good investment for some clinicians.

EXERCISES TO ACTIVATE THE SOCIAL ENGAGEMENT SYSTEM

Dr. Buczynski: For those who might struggle with some of our traditional therapies, are there other ways to activate the social engagement system that don't require face-to-face?

Dr. Porges: Yes, and that's a very good question. I pondered this for years, and that is why I developed the idea of using acoustic stimulation. I don't like intrusive therapy—that's my bias. I have a very deep respect for the individual and I want the individual to engage spontaneously, and if they spontaneously engage, then it is fine for me to respond.

I am theoretically committed to reciprocity and reciprocal interactions—I conceptualize reciprocal interactions as a neural exercise. If a person isn't engaging, you can stimulate spontaneous engagement behaviors with the use of prosodic voices. The use of prosodic voices also characterizes vocal music, and listening to vocal music may be helpful.

I am going to give you an example. A friend of mine who is a clinician was going to introduce me at a conference. Several hundred people were registered for the conference. I always thought that she was very energetic and didn't realize that she had severe anxiety about public speaking. She told me at the party on the night before that she was extremely anxious about introducing me in front of such a large audience. It is interesting what a drink or two at a party will enable someone to say. I told her not to worry: "I'll fix it."

On the following morning, at 10 minutes to nine—and the talk was scheduled to start at nine—she said to me, "Okay, Steve, fix it now." I looked at her and watched how she was speaking: She was speaking with very short phrases and gasping for breath between the short phrases. We all know people who talk like that—they are breathing on top of their phrases, and speaking this way conveys anxiety. In contrast to the long exhalations that promote calmness, a breathing strategy of short exhalations supports anxiety.

I said to her, "Extend the duration of your phrases. Add more words to your phrases before you take a breath." Initially, she couldn't do it; she couldn't get another word in. Finally, she got another word in, and then she got another, and then she was able to use a single breath for longer phrases. She started talking in a more engaging way. She then gave a wonderful and engaging introduction in which her voice conveyed a connectedness with the audience. She had a fear of public speaking—and she now uses this as a treatment for people with social anxiety.

There are ways to calm clients once we know specific physiological principles—and the physiological principle of calming was to get her to expand the durations of her exhalations while speaking. Neurophysiologically, the vagus has a greater calming effect on the heart during exhalation. But slow exhalations have another effect on social communication: As the vagal regulation of the heart increases, so does the vagal influence on the larynx and pharynx. The voice becomes more melodic and conveys cues to others of safety. Now she was able to speak in a clam state with a prosodic voice in front of 900 people.

This example provides a demonstration of a simple treatment strategy. Even if the client may have difficulties in social communication, if you are able to trigger the physiological state that supports social communication and calmness, then a variety of social behaviors spontaneously emerge from this neural platform. This occurs without trying to train or control the social behavior. It is different than traditional clinical strategies.

Dr. Buczynski: To what extent do you know exactly what she does with her patients who have social anxiety? How has she transferred or applied that?

Dr. Porges: Basically, she instructs her clients to extend the duration of their breaths while speaking—they are doing the behavior that used to get them anxious in a physiological state in which they are no longer anxious. Again, if you start extending the duration between breaths by expanding the number of words in each phrase, your physiology *is* calming down, and public speaking that was an anxiety-producing event is no longer—speaking in public is now occurring during a physiological state of calmness. There is another component of social engagement changing during this process. The voice is changing. The voice is no longer squeaky—the voice is now more melodic. The voice becomes pleasing to the individual.

Dr. Buczynski: This has to be done out loud. Could it be silent?

Dr. Porges: Having been a musician, a clarinetist, at one time in my youth, I would say that you can do a lot of things by visualizing—without actually doing the behavior. I could practice or rehearse without actually playing the instrument. If I had a concert and I had to play a solo, I would visualize and play the music in my head. There's a lot going on that can be both visualized and then merged with the actual behavior.

Dr. Buczynski: In terms of social anxiety conditions, I was wondering if, when people are frightened, their brain freezes and they can't think of what to say, and that would mean they wouldn't be able to extend their phrases—because they can't come up with what they want to say.

Could you have them count? Could you say, "Count as many numbers as you can before taking your next breath?"

Dr. Porges: What you did when you demonstrated that example was a gasp. You actually got into a physiological state similar to what you were trying to describe.

If you go with that type of mentalization, then people might be supporting the physiological state that may be incompatible with or counterproductive to what they want to do. If you have them exhale slowly and literally count the time of exhaling, they may then become more engaged. But if you do this type of gasping, you are going to get brain freezes—you are going to change your physiological state.

The model is simple: The difficulty occurs when you turn off the vagal control system and allow the sympathetic mobilization to occur, which now prepares you for flight/fight, not for social engagement.

I will give you another example. I had to give a talk at a conference on compassion. I was up there in front of a few hundred people, and they turned off the house lights. I started to talk, but talking without seeing people's faces is like falling into an abyss. I wasn't getting any feedback. I felt disconnected, which was kind of paradoxical, since this was a compassion conference. I had them turn the house lights back on; my comment was, "I get nothing out of giving a talk unless I can see people's faces."

What we are really saying is that part of the interaction that people have when they are fearful is that they are not getting anything back from the interaction—and there is so much to get back.

I guess we can tie this all together to what happens to people with trauma and the difficulty they have of no longer being able to use their interactions with another person to regulate their physiological state. Anxious people can't use their interaction with people to feel better about themselves. It is not cognitive—they are not feeling better about themselves because the strategies they use, the way they talk and the way they breathe, are supporting flight/fight behaviors, and they're not getting the benefits of reciprocal interactions, which recruit the social engagement system.

THE FUTURE OF TRAUMA TREATMENT

Dr. Buczynski: Stephen, where do you think the field of trauma treatment is going? What would you project or expect might be the most exciting parts? Where might we be in five years from now?

Dr. Porges: It is clearly going more body oriented—that you can see from all the clinicians that you interact with as well. I sit at a very interesting crossroads because I'm not a clinician. Not being a clinician, but being a scientist, who attempts to explain what clinicians do, has given me an entrée into diverse models of trauma treatment—including Somatic Experiencing developed by Peter Levine, Sensorimotor Psychotherapy developed by Pat Ogden, and the work of Bessel van der Kolk. These insightful clinicians have found Polyvagal Theory useful in explaining and providing a neurobiological explanation of their work.

The Polyvagal Theory provides the neurobiological linkage between body and brain and between body and psychological processes. We are moving toward an understanding of trauma as an adaptive reaction. It may be adaptive only for the initial reaction, although the features of reaction may literally get stuck and occur in inappropriate situations. All the treatment models seem to shift the threshold of shutting down and enable the client to be more socially engaged. The successful therapies seem to focus on shifting physiological state.

At the root of all of this—and this is where Polyvagal Theory is going—is an understanding of how our relationship with others enables the co-regulation of physiological state. My agenda is focused on the concept of safety through co-regulation as a biological imperative for humans. We can't survive well without interacting with another appropriate mammal. Trauma treatment may move to working with dogs, horses, and other mammals. But the issue is, how do we get the nervous system to spontaneously engage another? We need engagement to be healthy.

In the future, the use of pharmaceuticals for trauma will be greatly limited. Perhaps it will be focused on the acute reaction to the trauma. A change in dependence on pharmaceuticals will be difficult, because the medical profession is heavily pharmaceutically oriented. Psychiatrists are basically trained as applied psychopharmacologists with a belief that drugs can target the specific disorder that they are treating without the conceptualization that drugs affect neural feedback loops and affect many systems in the body.

I think the future has to move away from drugs for chronic treatment—although drugs might be useful for acute or emergency treatment. There has to be a greater respect for and understanding of the complete neural feedback loops; these feedback loops involve not only body–brain but people-to-people in the regulation of body and brain.

Dr. Buczynski: When we think about the treatment of trauma, it involves trust, and a lot of the Polyvagal Theory is connected to helping people feel safer. I was wondering whether your work is used much by marriage and family therapists or even couples' therapists.

Dr. Porges: This is an interesting question. I recently spoke at the Erickson Foundation Couples Conference. I was surprised to be invited. Next week, I'm doing the keynote plenary session for the American Group Psychotherapy Association. These are all new venues for me.

Dr. Buczynski: I'm thinking how one part of a couple

might be severely injured in some way and respond to stressful situations by withdrawing, and the other part of the couple might feel anxious and escalated, let's say—that's kind of a classic that we often see.

How could we teach the second person to behave in such a way that they could down-regulate the first person?

Dr. Porges: Yes, this is very difficult, and I say that because I am a husband, father, and mentor. Regulating one's own behavior when being triggered or cued is extraordinarily difficult. It is hard to be the observer when you are the participant, so that makes the couple's interaction really hard. Colleagues like Stanley Tatkin are very interested in videotaping and monitoring physiology during couples' therapy. He believes that understanding their own autonomic reactions while observing their own behaviors will be helpful to the couples in understanding their reactivity and even how the bias of their neuroception shifts.

By monitoring physiology, we might see the physiological state dynamically changing in the person. Now we are limited to a cognitive-behavioral worldview that doesn't totally respect what happens when our physiology goes awry.

If we monitor physiology during couples' therapy, we might see situations in which one member of the couple was triggered by a comment to have a rapid increase in heart rate and blood pressure and her body wanted to jump out of her skin. Her partner might be tempted to tell her, "Just calm down. Sit down. Don't worry." But given her physiological state, she probably would not be able to process the suggestion to calm down in a rational way—her neuroception might be biased to take all suggestions as hurtful and aggressive.

Suggesting that a mobilized individual calm down is not

respectful of the individual's limitations that physiological state might impose on behavior. We see this played out in terms of a misunderstanding of how our physiology impacts on both our own behavior and the behavior of our partners.

Dr. Buczynski: That's fascinating. The ideas you just shared, and even the ideas about social anxiety and the treatment of social anxiety, are *so* important.

6

THE FUTURE OF TRAUMA THERAPY: A POLYVAGAL PERSPECTIVE

Stephen W. Porges and Lauren Culp

Lauren Culp: What do you see happening and changing in the field of trauma treatment in the next five years?

Dr. Porges: Trauma creates problems for traditional therapeutic models. Traditional therapeutic models assume that most psychiatric disorders have a common neurobiological substrate linked to mechanisms mediating increased stress, fight/flight behavior, and sympathetic activation. All these constructs are related to states of hyperarousal that result in atypical behavioral regulation. However, clinicians realized after evaluating survivors of trauma that the neurobiological expression of their trauma is not always along a continuum of a highly mobilized defensiveness that we categorize as fight or flight reactions but often is expressed along a continuum of immobilization. These clients are experiencing not a hyperarousal with increased mobilization behaviors but something more like a total behavioral shutdown coupled with subjective experiences of despair and even features of dissociation that may reflect a motivation to disappear.

These behavioral and psychological symptoms have not fit well within classical models of defense, stress, and even clinical diagnoses of anxiety and depression. This lack of fit for the trauma survivor with current diagnostic and theoretical perspectives created an opportunity for the concepts that I had been developing with the Polyvagal Theory to contribute to our understanding of the biobehavioral reactions to trauma. As I developed the theory, I was trying to explain another basic defensive system used by mammals under extreme situations of life threat—a system of shutting down and immobilization. By not moving, mammals would not be detected by predators and, as a by-product of this strategy, heart rate may drop sufficiently to trigger a fainting response and consciousness would be lost, or for humans, states of dissociation may occur. This defense system could potentially foster safe outcomes for different mammalian species.

I had not thought of this defense strategy as a trauma reaction. I thought of it as a regression to a more primitive adaptive response that mammals shared with reptiles—and reptiles use as a primary defense system. But as I started to talk about the model and theory, the trauma community became very interested in the immobilization defense component of the Polyvagal Theory. If there is one group of professionals who intuitively understand and see the clinical application of the theory, it is the group of clinicians who treat trauma. For the trauma community, the Polyvagal Theory provides an understanding of the symptoms that are presented by survivors of trauma.

I have had interesting discussions with clinicians and survivors of severe trauma. These discussions inform my research. I learned that survivors of severe trauma often experienced states that traditional clinical theories couldn't explain. Many survivors of trauma felt that they were victims of the therapies being used in their treatments! I learned that the symptoms that they experienced did not make sense to them. I also learned that the clinical explanations did little to reassure them that they were on a path to healing. Many felt like they were crazy and could not understand their feelings and the psychological consequences of their trauma. Based on what I learned from both clinicians and individuals who had suffered severe trauma, I started to insert into my talks and workshops statements about trauma survivors learning to celebrate the success of their bodies in navigating and negotiating extraordinarily dangerous situations, like life threat. Basically, I wanted to infuse into their personal narrative a respect for the involuntary reactions of their nervous system, which put them into a physiological state that enabled them to survive.

Although their reaction to life threat may have put them into a state that enabled them to survive, it also created a problem. The problem was that the state that saved them was a state from which they could not easily get out of. Once in that state of shutdown, it was difficult for them to recover the behavioral state flexibility that defines resilience. These limitations become evident when the survivor is confronted with demands to socially interact. Under these demands, the survivor experiences an inability to socially interact that is greatly different from the comforting social interactions experienced before the trauma. Once we understand that the state that saved us is also a state that is currently limiting our ability to be social and feel good, we can still celebrate our body's successes.

When I talk to clinicians, I typically ask them, "What would happen if you told your clients, as opposed to demanding that they be more social, more interactive, 'Let's take a few moments now and celebrate what your body did'?" After making these statements in talks, I started getting emails back from clinicians about how demystifying reactions to trauma were in themselves healing. They told me that some of their clients were actually recovering, or at least improving in terms of their symptoms, once they lost a sense of fear of what their body was doing when they couldn't understand it. So, to make this statement simpler, I see the world of trauma moving away from trying to categorize all adaptive defense behaviors as if they were fight or flight and moving toward respecting the primitive defense systems that are extraordinarily successful in removing us from injury and pain. Once we respect the adaptive function of shutting down, therapy must address the important question: how do you move someone out of defensive states and into states in which they can interact with people and feel safer?

Lauren Culp: A close family member experienced a trauma of home invasion when he was asleep, and he now has PTSD. In addition to exploring the cognitive understanding of the experience with professionals, I used my experience as a massage therapist to use touch as a way to ground the person. What are your thoughts on the use of therapeutic touch?

Dr. Porges: In general, when people have experienced trauma, they may not easily be receptive to other people or easily be receptive to being touched. As a clinician, you have to be very sensitive to the client's vulnerabilities and find the window of opportunity to engage. Also, you have to be very sensitive to the client's reaction to your engagement behaviors.

I suggest that therapists be sensitive and detect cues when the client starts to loose resilience during the session. When this occurs the therapist needs to back off rather than push the client, which used to be part of some treatment models.

Lauren Culp: I hear you saying that it is important to stay very present with the cues of a patient who has experienced a form of trauma and to respect that individual's unique experience. As a clinician, I also try to find the strength-based areas where people have found their own tools to help themselves reorganize their experiences.

Dr. Porges: With trauma, it's not the event; it's the response to the event that is critical. To remind me I use the following phrase: "everyone's hell is their own." To me, this means that my judgments of the traumatic event are irrelevant to the client, and it is the client's response that determines the trajectory of outcome. Therefore, for situations that we may think are relatively benign, another individual's nervous system could respond to it as if it were a life-or-death situation. And, of course, when you have a home invasion, people might say, "Well, you are alive and not injured, so what are you concerned about?" In making that statement, they are not sensitive to the victim's bodily response to the violation. The critical point is that we must respect that our nervous system sometimes does what we want it to do, based upon voluntary behavior, and sometimes may functionally betray our intentions while attempting to save us.

I will describe my own personal experience of this type of body betrayal. Several years ago, I was getting an infusion for a heart checkup. The infusion catheter started to slip out of my arm, so I told the technician, and he moved the infusion catheter around to make sure it was appropriately inserted.

However, when he moved the catheter, it triggered afferent pathways associated with blood pressure regulation, and I passed out. His interpretation was that I was afraid. It had absolutely nothing to do with fear. It had to do with the fact that they triggered certain sensory receptors. The medical world interprets behavioral consequences, similar to the symptoms of trauma survivors, as psychological whether or not the behaviors, such as fainting, are physiological reflexes.

It is important, however, not to think that everything influencing our brain and consciousness occurs through a bottom-up model. We also have access to top-down circuits that enable us to use our cognitive functions to restructure and help us function, even though we may have experienced certain traumas or disruptions in our normal developmental trajectory.

As a species, we are fortunate that we have a large brain—we can use it to take in information and literally become our own parent, teacher, or therapist. As we take in new information, we modify our behavior and thoughts. This flexibility in our behavior and cognition enables us to be more resilient, flexible, and adaptive than if we remained constrained by our early childhood deficits and treat early disruptions and trauma as deterministic influences leading to failure. Having a good brain—having a big brain—we can now start talking about top-down mechanisms. This contrasts with my earlier points related to bottom-up mechanisms in which the actions and decisions of the brain may be subjugated to state shifts in the body.

Our brain can reorganize how our body feels. We can reinterpret, see things in a different way; we can shift disappointment and anger to a more respectful understanding that the people who may have failed us were merely trying to adapt under very difficult circumstances themselves. Many people cannot let go of the past and often attribute many of their current problems to their early experiences with poor parenting. They forget that their parents were children who may have experienced poor parenting and trauma. Often the individuals who blame their parents forget that they themselves are parents as well. They are now creating a transgenerational pathology in which their parenting is also compromised. Having a large brain allows us to understand that many of the features that may have been hurtful in the past may have been stimulated by some innocent adaptive behavior.

We are all extremely sensitive to disruptions in social interactions. For example, we have powerful visceral reactions if we are engaged in a conversation and then the person just walks away without terminating the social interaction. When this happens, our body cries out to tell us that something is wrong. This is a situation that we can't tolerate—it's a violation of an expectancy for a social interaction.

I have never heard anyone say, "Wow, this is really peculiar. Why should I be so upset?" Even sophisticated scientists and clinicians don't explain this type of behavior by considering that the person, due to physiological state change, might be expressing autistic-like behaviors. Rather, they assume motivation for the insensitive behavior of the person walking away. For example, we might think that the person who walked away doesn't like us, that the person doesn't value us, or that we are not important enough. We start confabulating, building a plausible model attributing a motivation to the behavior. We never step back and say—maybe this person is trying to adapt in a very complex social environment and doesn't have the neural resources to support social behavior.

I consider this an extremely important issue—that we have both bottom-up and top-down strategies. We have bottom-up strategies in which our body subjugates our brain and conveys feelings associated with adjustments to stress and danger that impact on our ability to perceive the world. But we also have top-down strategies that we can use to put ourselves into safe environments; then we can start to use this knowledge to deconstruct and demystify things that may have been hurtful to us.

Lauren Culp: In my clinical practice, I work with adult children of spectrum adults, from ADD to Asperger's, who with that new insight can create a shift in their current experience and understanding.

Dr. Porges: Yes! In telling the story of our own past, we are not the child anymore. We are the adult. It is a very interesting and rewarding approach. This is critical for people of my generation whose parents experienced world wars, the depression, and things we don't even think about in our culture today. We say, "Well, these people survived it." Of course, we should have been more understanding that a sense of safety and security was not conveyed with their survival.

Lauren Culp: I am wondering about your work in schools and in the field of autism.

Dr. Porges: I was involved in designing the building for a school for autism that is run by the Easter Seals Foundation in Chicago. The school had to have certain features. One important feature was that the classrooms should be quiet. We worked on reducing background noise and providing lots of ambient light that would not be glaring. The windows are 5 feet off the ground and do not provide visual stimulation that is distracting. The rooms are illuminated with indirect lights that remove glare. The rooms have excellent sound attenuation, with sound-absorbing ceilings and carpeted floors. We did this because many individuals with autism are hypersensitive and have lower thresholds to react to sound and light. They may even have a dampened pupillary reflex—their eyes may be more dilated and not rapidly constrict to increases in illumination. Basically, many children with autism are in a chronic physiological state of mobilization. When in this state, their pupils will be more dilated and their middle ear muscles will not be working as well. When the pupils are dilated, there is a hypersensitivity to light. When the middle ear muscles are not working well, there is a hypersensitivity to sound. We incorporated this understanding of physiological state on sensitivities to light and sound into the design.

Next, we tried to change the culture of the school. This is a really interesting issue. In most school systems autism is treated by special education professionals. There are a variety of other supportive disciplines such as speech and language therapy, occupational therapy, and physical therapy, but basically special education teachers deliver educational services to children with autism and other developmental disabilities. But, in general, special education strategies were not designed for autism. They were designed for individuals experiencing learning delays, who don't have hypersensitivities and who don't have state regulation issues. The imposition of special education models on a population that is behaviorally reactive creates a major problem, because the special education model assumes that behavior is voluntary and not an emergent spontaneous property of a physiological state.

I would like to bring new methods into educational institutions to improve autistic children's emotional, behavioral, and cognitive availability. These methods would deviate from the special education strategy of behavior modification and exposure to traditional academic disciplines. Instead, I would like to apply methods that provide neural exercises to improve biobehavioral state regulation. First, I want to apply the Listening Project Protocol (see Chapter 2 and 3), which we successfully implemented in our laboratory. The Listening Project Protocol uses computer-altered music and functions to reduce auditory hypersensitivities and calm behavior and physiology (see Porges et al. 2013, 2014). The intervention helps place the child in a physiological state from which social engagement behaviors may spontaneously emerge. Second, I want to use biofeedback procedures using breathing strategies to calm and improve heart rate regulation. By improving heart rate regulation, the child will have a resource to calm and down-regulate the shifts in physiological state that are manifested in classroom-disruptive behaviors such as tantrums and oppositional behaviors. The successful outcomes of both methods are based on the assumption that if the child is calmer and less reactive and defensive, the dynamics of the educational environment will change and the child will become more available for learning and social behavior.

Auditory hypersensitivities are an important problem in the management of autism. Approximately 60 percent of individuals with autism have auditory hypersensitivities. This number may be an underestimate, since parents often think that if their children don't put their fingers in their ears, they don't have auditory hypersensitivities. Once I asked a parent if his autistic child had auditory hypersensitivities. He responded that his son used to, but this was no longer a problem. Being curious, I asked how he had fixed the problem. He told me he taught his son not to put his fingers in his ears. Functionally, the parent had trained away the behavior, which was the observable window to an adaptive response to the painful reaction to acoustic stimulation. Without the behavior, the parent no longer had access to the child's feelings of discomfort and pain.

Although the child with auditory sensitivities was making an adaptive adjustment to the loud stimulation by putting his fingers in his ears, the behavior was disruptive to the parents and the teachers. The parents and the teachers felt that placing fingers in the ears signaled that these children did not want to listen to them. The parents and teachers did not consider that the sounds were overwhelming to the child because the sounds were not overwhelming to them. Again, it is the issue of respecting the physiological state of the other and respecting that the sensory world of the other may differ from yours. This respect for another person's sensory world appears to be limited in the medical and educational communities. If the culture were to respect individual differences in how the nervous system responds, developmental trajectories could be improved. This is a goal of our research.

An important issue for communities is that schools, in a way, warehouse challenged children. Even though an enormous amount of money is spent with good intentions by school districts for the treatment and education of children with autism and other developmental disabilities, the outcomes from these treatment models frequently do not result in the child developing sufficient skills and competencies to be integrated into society. These limited outcomes don't mean that the outcomes of autistic children are always poor, but in general, the educational experience for autistic children is stressing for them and for their families and educators. I want to create an environment where science not only informs practice, but practice informs science. In this case, practice is informing us that the educational experience of the autistic child is neurophysiologically stressing.

Academicians, scientists, and clinicians each have a unique perspective on autism. However, these professionals are less sensitive to the fact that the various symptoms associated with being autistic can disrupt the lives of entire families. For example, auditory hypersensitivities disrupt families; they limit where the hypersensitive child can be and affect daily activities within the home. This is disruptive to the lives of many of these families, yet this is not a domain that scientists investigating autism want to study. They don't want to study it, in part, because funding agencies don't want to support research in this area. And funding agencies don't support this area of research because it is not specific to autism. Funding agencies are looking for the neurobiological signature or the genetic signature of autism. They won't find a signature for autism, because the diagnosis is represented by a heterogeneity of the behavioral and neurophysiological features.

Auditory hypersensitivities are also observed in people who have been traumatized. There may be a common core of clinical problems in several psychiatric disorders, because a retraction of the neural regulation of the social engagement system occurs when the physiological state is in a defensive mode. A retraction of the social engagement system would result in auditory hypersensitivities as well as the flat facial affect found in many clinical disorders.

Another problem with autism research is that virtually all of the research is done in a laboratory setting. Where is the diagnosis being made? Diagnoses are made in the clinic. A clinical environment, similar to a laboratory, may trigger defensive behaviors, which will result in limiting the autistic individual's functional range of behavior. In the clinic or the laboratory, you don't know whether the observed differences between autistic and nonautistic individuals are due to defensive reactions to the environment or truly to a characteristic of the individual. The best way to understand autism is to see the child in a familiar environment. So I decided to move my research on autism from my laboratory in a research center to a school for autism. By creating a laboratory in the school, where the child was familiar with the context, the tremendous uncertainty of the child coming to a new environment to be tested or evaluated would be reduced.

We see wonderful things happen during the Listening Project Protocol. For many children, by the time they finish the intervention, they spontaneously embrace the staff and give them hugs and want to come back. The laboratory setting within the school for autism is supportive, friendly, and calming; it is not stressing to them. Juxtapose the laboratory within a school with placing a child with autism in an MRI within a hospital setting. I have always wondered which autistic individuals could go into an MRI, because many of them have auditory hypersensitivities and of course would not like being constrained. Might we be misinformed by fMRI research on autism by the selectivity of the subset of individuals diagnosed with autism who are able to tolerate the MRI?

Lauren Culp: One of my teenage patients used to spin when he was little and now flaps/flicks his hands when he is stressed. What do you think about that?

Dr. Porges: Does he rock? Does he like to swing? Swinging in a head-to-toe direction stimulates the receptors involved in blood pressure regulation and helps organize the vagal system, which is calming, and might reduce flapping. When a child flaps his hands, he is expressing a mobilization reaction within a social context. He is not running away. He is just flapping his hands. Often parents get upset when a child flaps and try to extinguish the behavior. So instead of flapping, the child might pace. One child that I knew wore out the carpet in his bedroom because his mother did not want him to flap. I view flapping as an adaptive mobilization behavior within a social context. Rather than being fully out of control, you are just flapping your hand.

One of the simplest techniques to help calm and help self-regulate is swinging. This might include swinging on a porch swing or a glider or a rocking chair. Porch swings were common before we became an air-conditioned society. In the first half of the 20th century, houses frequently had porches and couples used to swing together as part of a social engagement strategy. They are not very popular anymore, but they had a function. Swinging, in a sense, used behavior to modify physiological state and functioned as a biobehavioral intervention. Swinging is calming. Swings may help an autistic child to self-regulate. Rocking on an exercise ball may provide an efficient method of stimulating the sacral afferents of the parasympathetic nervous system. These afferents transmit information to the brainstem and increase parasympathetic tone. Thus, rocking on an exercise ball may provide an alternative portal to stimulate central regulation of the vagus.

Lauren Culp: In general, where have we been in the last five years and where do you see us going in the next five years with interpersonal neurobiology—the brain, mind, and relationships?

Dr. Porges: The first point is that it is extremely important for scientists who study the nervous system to be informed by the clinical community. There are major gaps between laboratory scientists and clinical practitioners. Research models and neural models of various disorders often miss some of the major features seen in the clinical world. This gap between research and the clinic even expands into the realm of clinical research. In medical schools, scientists, who are also licensed practitioners, conduct much of the clinical research. These clinical researchers spend most of their time conducting research and not seeing patients. However, often the clinical features observed within the laboratory are different from what is seen within the clinic. From a personal perspective, I have always found talking to clinicians a way of informing me of what the real problems are as opposed to scientific research being a platform to pontificate—a way of viewing the client.

Where are things going in the next five years? I am going to tell you something that you might not expect to hear. I think we have been living in a world that has become both brain-centric and now is becoming gene-centric in our desire to try to understand mental health problems and to optimize the human experience. I think, in focusing on brain structures and brain functions in the way that has been done, we miss one of the major points that clinicians are extraordinarily aware of, and that is the importance of bodily feelings and how they regulate and often subjugate our ability to access higher brain processes, including the higher psychological processes involved in thinking, loving, and socially interacting. As we have become victim to the products of the technologies that quantify genetics and brain function, we have minimized the important realm of sickness behaviors that permeate all aspects of the body, and we have become focused on specific brain areas or genetic polymorphisms.

If we think in terms of symptomology, whether we are talking about psychiatric symptoms, behavioral problems, or even just physical health symptoms, most of the symptoms are actually in the periphery. The nervous system is not solely a brain independent of the body, but a brain–body nervous system. The future of interpersonal neurobiology is in understanding that our nervous system expands throughout our entire body and is functionally responding to the interactions with other human beings as well. I see the future of interpersonal neurobiology as leading to a greater understanding of how social interactions and social support, through a therapist, a family member, or a friend, can facilitate physical and mental health.

Lauren Culp: You've shared so much for us to chew on. Thanks for taking this time with us.

7

SOMATIC PERSPECTIVES ON PSYCHOTHERAPY

Stephen W. Porges and Serge Prengel

Serge Prengel: Based on your writings, it appears that you have paid a lot of attention to the nervous system.

Dr. Porges: My research has focused on how neural regulation of physiological state influences behavior and how these mechanisms are related to how we interact socially. In fact, even when I was young, I was curious about how we regulate our behavioral state in the presence of others. Although the question originated in my youth, it has been only during the past decade or two that I realized that this ability was a core issue in many aspects of mental health and had a great impact on quality of life.

Serge Prengel: So it's not just an individual pursuit of understanding how to regulate yourself.

Dr. Porges: Well, it actually may have started out as a personal pursuit, and then somehow it blended into my research questions and co-opted my research skills. My research started off addressing a more esoteric question related to the parameters of physiological reactions that would enable efficient information processing. Then, as I was developing my research skills, I began to think about underlying physiological processes, not just physiological indicators or correlates of efficient cognitive processing. I started to ask questions about bodily feelings and emotions. Gradually, I started to ask questions about regulating bodily feelings and emotions in the presence of others and started to investigate the interesting dialectic between how the nervous system mediates our visceral feelings and how these feelings are greatly influenced by social interactions.

Serge Prengel: How does our nervous system interplay with our visceral feelings?

Dr. Porges: Although the important role that the nervous system plays in regulating our visceral state is a relevant question for people interested in body psychotherapy, it is not acknowledged in the prevalent models, theories, and therapies used and taught in psychology and psychiatry. Psychology and psychiatry primarily use top-down models that conceptualize emotions and affective processes as central phenomena and minimize the role of the body in these experiences. Consistent with these models, even anxiety may be viewed as a "brain" process without a visceral manifestation. Fortunately, there are clinicians, including many body psychotherapists, who have an appreciation of the importance of the bidirectional communication between the brain and the body. For example, sensory information travels from the body to the brain and influences how we respond to the world. And brain processes can influence our viscera via the cognitive and affective processes related to our perspective of the world and our reactions to various features of the environment. This bidirectional and interactive notion of how our nervous system regulates our viscera in a complex social environment, although intuitive, is neglected or minimized by much of clinical medicine, including psychiatry.

Serge Prengel: Feelings don't happen by themselves in some kind of isolated sphere, but there is a bidirectionality between our bodily feelings and cognitive thoughts.

Dr. Porges: Absolutely. The strategy of subjugating feelings and the preeminence of cognitive processes follow a long tradition in Western culture of emphasizing thoughts at the expense of feelings. For example, we can go back to Descartes and discuss how his philosophy structured mind–body dualism. Descartes states in French, "*Je pense donc je suis,*" which when translated into English is "I think, therefore I am." However, let's speculate about consequences if Descartes used a different phrase, "*Je me sens donc je suis,*" or "I feel; therefore I am." Note the use of the reflexive form of the verb "to feel," which literally would translate into "I feel myself, therefore I am." If he had used this phrase, he would have been emphasizing the bodily feelings that parallel and contribute to our emotions and not how it feels to touch an object.

In English, we use the same word to describe the sensations arising from within our body and the sensations we experience while touching an object. Unfortunately, the personal experience of feelings within the body was not part of the equation for Descartes. But imagine how our treatment of people would have evolved if that is what Descartes had really said. Where would we be today in terms of a historical trajectory of what it is to be a human? Instead, based on Descartes, our culturally based philosophies have adopted the premise that to be a good human, we have to depress or reject our visceral feelings to enable our good brain, our smart brain, to express its potential. Physical and mental illness may be a consequence of an adherence to Descartes's dictum. Thus, not respecting the body's own responses and filtering visceral feelings, over time, may contribute to illness by dampening the bidirectional neural feedback between brain and body.

Serge Prengel: It might be helpful to our listeners to discuss how we experience visceral feelings and how they connect to our cognitions and what may happen if there are problems in either expressing visceral feelings or if there is a disconnect between our cognitions and the rest of the body.

Dr. Porges: Well, it's really quite interesting. I am actually writing about this now. I have been working on the impact of safety on our ability to access various attributes of our nervous system. It is important to understand that feeling safe is a prerequisite for our ability to be creative and to solve and implement solutions for difficult problems. Our culture takes a paradoxical perspective in defining safety. We focus on words and cognitive representations and minimize bodily responses and feelings to define safety. As professionals and academics, we think that we can use our cognitive skills to define safety. Yet being safe is really the body's response to the environment.

Basically, educational and socialization processes in our culture are working very hard to dismiss the body's responses to environmental features. If we observe children in a classroom, we note a variety of behavioral features that illustrate that some children are safe and can sit comfortably in the same environment that triggers in other children the hypervigilant behaviors characterizing a lack of safety. Moreover, the children who are chronically monitoring for cues of danger in the classroom are frequently the same children who have difficulties in learning, while those who feel safe can attend to the teacher and learn efficiently. Unfortunately, the traditional classroom model for education assumes that if some children can perform well in a classroom, every child should.

Our society treats the behaviors of individuals who are behaviorally or viscerally reactive to slight changes in stimulation as bad or defective. In fact, we reinforce this "moral" conceptualization with labels such as developmental "disability" or mental "retardation" or attention "deficit." Society assumes that children should be able to voluntarily turn these behaviors off and that if they can't, then they are defective.

Rather than investigating and understanding that there is a neural substrate underlying the observed range of individual differences, we basically convey to these children that the behaviors are bad even if the behaviors are involuntary. Alternatively, the educational process could celebrate some of the unique sensitivities that people have. However, this seldom occurs and leads into the world of trauma treatment in which many of our colleagues work.

The world of trauma is primarily about bodily responses and reactions. In some cases, the behavioral pattern and neural regulation of autonomic state changes dramatically following trauma. These changes can be so great that the behavioral features may appear to represent a totally different person who no longer can relate to others or interact in the same world. Since the behaviors of the traumatized individual do not conform to the expectations of typical social interactions, the traumatized individual often feels that they are inadequate or cannot do things correctly. These feelings of inadequacy may be driven by societal expectations and even through the evaluative feedback during clinical sessions. For example, therapeutic strategies may provide a continuous dialogue of evaluation, often emphasizing deficiencies in the hope of triggering voluntary control of more prosocial behaviors. However, the continuous evaluation of their behavior may push the client further and further into defensive strategies.

Serge Prengel: I want to slow it down a little bit, because there's so much information in what you are saying. For instance, children are exposed in school to a preimposed model that's almost a mechanical model of functioning. Children are treated like machines. If one machine functions a certain way, then similar machines are expected to have the same behavior regardless of any individual differences in physiological arousal or threshold to be reactive to environmental stimulation.

Dr. Porges: To reemphasize what you very succinctly described, we treat children in school as if they are learning machines, and the success of school is really defined by what information we are able to program into that machine. We don't respect the important need of visceral state regulation as a skill set, which serves as a prerequisite or a neurophysiological platform upon which learning and social behavior are dependent. The development of skills focused on improving visceral state regulation are not part of the curriculum. Thus, opportunities to exercise neural systems to improve neural regulation of physiological state, which in turn would support a more efficient expression of social behavior, are not available or are minimized in the prevalent educational models.

These points become obvious when studying challenged individuals, like autistic children. Interestingly, with autistic children, the basic treatment model is a special education model. This model builds on learning theory and uses reinforcement and repetition in the establishment of skills.

Unfortunately, the "learning model" does not incorporate an important feature of autism that is shared with other clinical disorders—the inability to regulate visceral state in the presence of others. In contrast, the prevalent treatment models force the individual to regulate in a context that may make learning inefficient.

Serge Prengel: Sensitive and effective therapists are very careful to realize that clients cannot change unless they're in a regulated state. Unfortunately, treatment models often impose a less sensitive model on children and try to force-feed them when they haven't learned the basics of regulation.

Dr. Porges: In addition, the child's nervous system might not be sufficiently developed to regulate in a complex setting. So rather than incorporating an understanding of how the nervous system regulates behavioral state, we try to use laws of learning by ramping up the motivation through punishment or reward to change behavior when perhaps the neural mechanisms are not sufficiently developed or atypical. Thus, these strategies are, at best, inefficient.

In my talks, I often discuss underlying visceral state as biasing or distorting our reactions to the world. I use a slide of a traffic signal with green, yellow, and red lights. Each light represents a different physiological state. The green light represents a physiological state associated with safety. The yellow light represents a physiological state associated with danger. The red light represents a physiological state associated with life threat. To the left of the traffic light signal is an "S" for the environmental stimulus. To the right of the traffic light, I put an "R" for the individual's response to the stimulus. Thus, the response to a common stimulus is qualified by the physiological state. The same stimulus in the environment might produce qualitatively different responses based on the physiological state of the individual at the time the stimulus is presented.

Serge Prengel: As you describe this interaction between cognitive processes, reactions, and the ability to regulate our emotions and our reaction to fear, it feels that you're giving a great example of what you said earlier about how that's a different conception of what it's like to be human.

Dr. Porges: Basically, I am questioning the goals of our institutions. Are the goals of our institutions to educate people with more information, or are our goals to make people better able to reciprocally interact and to regulate each other to feel good? This goes back to Descartes's dictum, which has led us down a track of more thinking, expansive cognitive skills, and cognitively defined "smarter people." However, despite this enhanced level of smartness, we have become literally ignorant about what our bodies really need to feel good.

Serge Prengel: Maybe we should talk about what our bodies need to feel good—how visceral reactions work, the defining features of the neural circuits connecting the viscera and the nervous system. This is important, because often people discuss being in their body, and there is an almost mystical or metaphysical quality to the body versus thought. And as I think you described, in the process itself, there is a sense of that bottom-up quality.

Dr. Porges: I like to say that a goal of society is to be able to immobilize without fear. This statement might initially sound strange. However, when you think about it, isn't immobilization without fear really a goal of therapy? You don't want your clients to remain "tightly wrapped," anxious and defensive. You want your clients to be able to sit quietly, to be embraced without fear, to be hugged and to hug others, to conform physically when embraced, and to be reciprocal in their relationships. If a client is tightly wrapped, with tense muscles and in a highly activated sympathetic nervous system state, the client is conveying this state of defensiveness to others. A state characterized by tense muscles and sympathetic excitation is an adaptive state that prepares an individual to move or fight. This state unambiguously conveys to others that it is not safe to be in close proximity to this person.

This may be a good time to emphasize some of the neural circuits that regulate the autonomic nervous system. The first point is related to the information flowing from our body to the brain. The autonomic nervous system is extraordinarily important in conveying information about our viscera to our brain. The vagus, the largest nerve in the autonomic nervous system and the major nerve of the parasympathetic nervous system, is primarily a sensory nerve with about 80 percent of its fibers beings sensory. The vagus is continuously conveying a tremendous amount of information about the status of peripheral organs to specific nuclei in the brainstem. The sensory information from the viscera does not share the same specificity as tactile stimulation or other sensory information going up the spinal cord. Visceral feelings are generally diffuse, so the actual labeling becomes difficult, and the diffuse feelings often "color" our perceptions and reactions to social interactions.

The second point is related to the motor control of the autonomic nervous system. In fact, the traditional definition of the autonomic nervous system focused solely on the motor components, the neural pathways in the periphery to the target organs, and the target organs in the viscera. Important characteristics of the vagus have been neglected by this focus on the motor portion of the vagus without examining the brainstem areas in which the vagal pathways originate. Specifically, the fact that the vagus has two functionally distinct branches with different functions is often neglected.

Most individuals are taught that the autonomic nervous system has two components: a sympathetic nervous system associated with fight/flight behavior and a parasympathetic nervous system, which is primarily associated with a cranial nerve known as the vagus, associated with growth, health, and restoration. This presentation of the autonomic nervous system suggests that the sympathetic and parasympathetic components are antagonistic. While casting the autonomic nervous system as reflecting paired antagonism is at times useful, it is not completely accurate.

Although we often use the construct of autonomic balance, the autonomic nervous system seldom functions as a balance system and is more likely to react to challenges in the environment in a hierarchical manner. It is this contradiction of conceptualizing the components of the autonomic nervous system either as a "balance" or a "hierarchical" system that served to motivate me to develop the Polyvagal Theory. In the traditional view of the autonomic nervous system, the sympathetic nervous system is involved in fight and flight responses while the parasympathetic nervous system is involved in health, growth, and restoration. However, the Polyvagal Theory actually describes a second defense system in addition to the fight/flight system, which everyone is familiar with and requires sympathetic and adrenal responses. The theory identifies a second defense system. The second system is linked not to mobilized fight/flight behaviors but to immobilization, shutting down, fainting, and dissociating. This second defense system is a life threat system that is frequently observed in small rodents such as mice.

When a cat picks up the mouse, the mouse immobilizes and looks dead. This is not a voluntary behavior; the mouse is not deciding to play dead. Rather, the life threat features of the cat trigger an ancient neural circuit that is frequently used by reptiles as a defense system. Since reptiles' small brains do not need much oxygen, they can immobilize and even hold their breath for long periods. However, this is not an option for mammals, which need massive amounts of oxygen to support their larger brains. This shutdown immobilization response is mediated by vagal mechanisms. In fact, fainting is called vasovagal syncope, which acknowledges the potent disruptive effect of the vagus on our normal cardiovascular function.

Thus, we have a vagal response pattern that is not consistent with the health, growth, and restoration responsibilities that have been associated with the vagus and the parasympathetic nervous system for decades. The vagal defense system has literally been written out of the literature on the autonomic nervous system. Without a "vagal defense system," autonomic function fits nicely into a simple paired antagonism model in which the sympathetic component supports fight/flight behaviors and is competing with the parasympathetic component that supports health, growth, and restoration.

The inclusion of a vagal defense system challenges this simple model of autonomic balance and forces us to reconceptualize the adaptive reactions of the autonomic nervous system as reflecting three hierarchical components. This functional hierarchy mirrors the phylogeny of these autonomic components in vertebrates. The oldest vagal system is mediated by an unmyelinated vagus that originates in the brainstem in an area known as the dorsal nucleus of the vagus. The 'old' vagal system is shared with virtually all vertebrates. In mammals, the system, when triggered as a defense system, inhibits breathing, slows heart rate, and promotes reflexive defecation. However, in safe contexts, the system supports the subdiaphragmatic organs to promote health, growth, and restoration. The sympathetic nervous system, when triggered as a defense system, functionally inhibits the old vagus, stops digestion, and diverts energy resources from visceral support to mobilization.

The phylogenetically most recent autonomic system represents myelinated vagal motor pathways. This component of the vagus is unique to mammals and originates in a brainstem structure that is linked to the muscles of the face and head. Now we understand that when people smile, when they are happy, and when their voice has prosodic features reflected in variations in vocal intonation like a mother's lullaby, they are able to focus, to hear, and to understand vocal communication. Functionally, the myelinated vagus calms us, efficiently processes our cardiovascular and metabolic needs, and actively inhibits states of arousal associated with the sympathetic nervous system.

Serge Prengel: So the vagus, or the two parts of the vagus nerve, are in fact, on the one hand, the most ancient and also the most recent parts of our evolution.

Dr. Porges: The two components of our vagus are mirroring the extreme features of vertebrate evolution of the autonomic nervous system.

Serge Prengel: And the fight/flight is in between.

Dr. Porges: Yes, with the sympathetic nervous system supporting fight/flight behaviors. I have developed a simple narrative to describe the unique autonomic and behavioral features of mammals. As mammals evolved, their survival was dependent on satisfying a need to interact for nursing and for other forms of social interactions and group behaviors linked to obtaining food, reproducing, playing, and supporting general safety needs. The new mammalian vagus was able to turn off defense systems. However, to balance the needs of social interaction with the needs for safety, it is necessary to know when to turn the defenses off and when to turn the defenses back on. In our society, this is a major issue. When do we turn off our defenses? When are we safe to be in the arms of another? When are we safe to go to work? When are we safe to go to sleep? Clients often have issues about not feeling safe with others. They have difficulties turning off their defense systems. They can't be hugged. They have sleeping disorders. They have gut disorders. All these symptoms are features of the autonomic nervous system that can only occur when the newer myelinated vagal system isn't making us feel safe by appropriately regulating the sympathetic and unmyelinated vagal components of the autonomic nervous system.

Serge Prengel: So, to effectively use our evolutionary heritage, our newest vagal circuit needs to effectively regulate the older circuits.

Dr. Porges: Yes. I'm starting to link physical and mental health vulnerabilities to specific neural structures that define the differences between reptiles and mammals. During this transition, a myelinated vagus evolved, the defense strategies became more focused on fight behaviors, and the immobilization defense system was minimized. It was minimized because immobilization is potentially lethal to mammals, who have a very high oxygen need. Our common ancestor with modern reptiles had features similar to a tortoise. The primary defense system of the tortoise is immobilization.

When we inquire about the experiences of traumatized individuals, we learn that many of them have experienced a profound and unexpected immobilization. By explaining the vagal defense system and how the unmyelinated vagus supports an ancient defense system to life threat, we can be very helpful in demystifying the responses that traumatized individuals experienced. Providing an explanation that life threat has triggered an ancient response circuit, which may have reorganized how the autonomic nervous system regulates physiological state, may help the client understand the changes in their day-to-day functioning.

Serge Prengel: So we are really talking about the fact that, in a way, the stronger the stress, the more we tend to regress to a very archaic form of survival.

Dr. Porges: But this has to deal with our definition of stress. If we interpret your use of stress as challenges to survival, the model fits well. As the "stress" imposes limits on our ability to escape the stress and reach a state of safety, then our physiology adjusts. This model places an emphasis on context and the nervous system's detection and interpretation of threat in the local environment. Our physical context interacts with our physiological state to determine the options we have to deal with stressors and challenges. We will flee or fight if we have an opportunity to escape or to defend ourselves. To support these adaptive mobilization strategies, we stimulate our sympathetic nervous system. But if we are locked in a room or being held down, we have very few options. Under these difficult and extremely dangerous and often life-threatening conditions, we might reflexively faint or immobilize in terror and slip into a dissociative state. These defensive behaviors are dependent on a phylogenetically older circuit.

As an example, a CNN news segment (see Chapter 2) illustrated an airplane having difficulty in landing. Although the situation looked precarious, the plane landed safely. After the plane landed, a reporter interviewed a woman and asked her how she felt during the landing. Her response was, "Feel? I passed out." Her response was neurophysiologically similar to the experience of the mouse in the jaws of a cat. It is obvious that there is an adaptive function to a fear-induced immobilization response in which the individual is no longer conscious or in the "here and now." Although the trigger for fainting is associated with mild hypoxia due to a massive drop in blood pressure, the defense response strategy has adaptive features by raising pain thresholds so that if you are going to be injured, you will not feel the pain. And, if you survive, hopefully you'll be fine; at least you will be alive. The real issue related to understanding the "shutdown" response as an adaptive defense reaction is to respect the responses that our body may automatically employ to protect us from pain and to save our lives. We need to acknowledge the positive attributes of the shutdown and not be angry at our body that we lost ability to fight and immobilized.

Serge Prengel: So we are coming back to what it's like to be human and to have that embodied experience.

Dr. Porges: The embodied experience is critical to humans, because interacting with others is critical for human survival. Throughout the entire human life span, humans are dependent on others. Starting with birth, infants require nursing and caregiving. As we mature, the interactions shift from safety and food to facilitating our physiological state, which we experience as emotional and behavioral regulation through our social interactions with friends and loved ones. The main point is that humans require interactions with others to develop and to optimize their potential. Several biological disciplines discuss similar processes within the construct of "symbiotic regulation." I think we are now in a good position to use this construct from a biobehavioral perspective to explain several aspects of how human social interactions facilitate neurobiological processes. Through expanding this construct, we can see how we reciprocally send cues to each other's nervous systems. Social interactions are characterized by continuously transmitting cues of safety or danger and whether it is safe to be held in the arms of another or to retreat and protect ourselves. I have used the term "neuroception" to explain this dynamic and interactive process.

Serge Prengel: You have paid attention to that in terms of the mechanisms through which we have evolved to experience love and attachment.

Dr. Porges: I have learned about these mechanisms from clinical populations that express difficulties in social connectedness. HIV patients provide an interesting example to elaborate on this point. In studying HIV patients, I have learned that often their caregivers feel unloved and frequently get angry attending to the needs of the infected individual. Parents of autistic children often report the same feelings and experiences. In both examples, although they often report feeling unloved, what they really are expressing is that the HIV-infected individual or the autistic child is not contingently responding to them with appropriate facial expressivity, eye gaze, and intonation in their voices. In both cases, the individual being cared for is behaving in a machinelike manner, and the caregivers feel disengaged and emotionally disconnected. Functionally, their physiological responses betray them, and they feel insulted. Thus, an important aspect of therapy is to deal not solely with the patient, but to also include the social context in which the patient lives with a focus on the parent–child or caregiver–client dyad. This will ensure that the parents or the caregivers will learn to understand their own responses as a natural physiological response.

Unfortunately, caregivers and parents often attribute motivation to the disengaging behavior. This creates problems. Similar to the frequent responses of teachers in schools, who become angry and aggressive when students disengage by turning away, parents and caregivers often justify their anger and abusiveness to the challenged child or individual.

Serge Prengel: Can we override our reflexive reactions?

Dr. Porges: We can attempt to override these reactions. However, this is very hard to do. In some of the workshops I have conducted, I have tried a simple experiential to illustrate this point. I call the experiential "the reluctant therapist." In the reluctant therapist, I create triads in which workshop participants rotate through three roles: therapist, client, and observer. In the experiential, the therapist is instructed to gaze-avert and turn away while the client is talking. The interesting point of the experiential is that the individual in the client role frequently gets very angry at the therapist. This occurs even though the client knew that the therapist was role-playing and instructed to turn away and disengage. In the experiential, the observer is uninvolved and has the responsibility to be objective and to report how the behavioral cues trigger massive behavioral and state shifts. When the participants rotate through the three roles, the reactions are reliably replicated. It's really quite amazing how easily our body changes state when someone disengages or engages with us.

Serge Prengel: That's the powerful part. Even knowing it, even in a role-play situation, social engagement has such a hold on us that we really cannot easily disengage from it.

Dr. Porges: It is quite amazing. In therapeutic settings, clinicians may deal with couples with different "engagement" resources. For example, if one member of the couple has a trauma history that may be manifested in state regulation issues and accompanied with gaze averting and turning away from the other during confrontations or even during more positive social interactions, what is the partner's response to this? Often their response is simply to get angry.

Serge Prengel: There is something that feels very nice about deconstructing the mechanisms of what happens in an interaction and the importance of helping others not to take these things personally, helping them to diminish the attribution of blame, helping them reduce the layers of interpretation that are a block to people functioning effectively with others.

Dr. Porges: I totally agree. I think we live in a world that attempts to attribute motivation to every behavior and to place an evaluative dimension of good or bad on the behavior. I use the term "moral veneer" as the feature in our society that pushes us to evaluate behavior as good or bad and not to see the adaptive function of the behavior as regulating physiological and behavioral state.

When I talk to clinicians, I used to use an example of an instance where a boss or chairperson didn't look at the clinician. I wanted to elicit a visceral feeling of being marginalized. I had expected interpretations ranging from the boss didn't like them or that they were not important enough for the boss to attend to them. I noticed that many in the audience had blank faces and could not relate to what I was describing. Then I realized that most clinicians don't work for anyone. They don't work for anyone because these disengagement behaviors, which they often interpret as evaluative, did not make them feel good. However, my life has been in the academic world, a social environment in which administrators and many colleagues tend to have limited social skills.

However, the point I am trying to make is that most of the behaviors that we label as social skills are not learned. Rather, most of these behaviors appear to be more an emergent property of our biological state than they are "skills" in social learning.

There are people who make good eye contact, are curious about others, and have a broad range of facial expressivity. These people are also reciprocal in their social interactions. To maintain this reciprocity, they are literally throwing obvious and often subtle cues at each other. These cues have the potential to make the other person feel safe. When the cues are effective, the other person returns the cues through facial expressions and vocalizations. The face appears more alive, more expressive; the intonation of the voice becomes more prosodic; and the physical distance between the two people is often reduced as the physical space starts to approximate the reduced psychological distance. I am sure that you have observed this within your clinical practices.

Serge Prengel: We do when we are in the middle of clinical practice. We really pay attention to it and are very aware of it, but of course we react as human beings. We have just as much difficulty as everybody else paying attention to it.

Dr. Porges: My personal test of these qualities has occurred as a father and as a mentor for my students. How do we react to our children or students when they start throwing cues at you? I learned to step back and think about their physiological state. What if they haven't eaten? What if they haven't slept? What if they have major problems at home? If events and contexts compromise their ability to recruit the neural circuit that supports safety and social interactions, the interaction is going to be very challenging. So the ability to be engaging, expressive, and understanding is going to be limited. We can generalize to our entire culture and identify features that would interfere with access to the neural circuit supporting social engagement. Remember that our culture is not structured to promote personal safety. It is a culture that unambiguously states that we can't work hard enough, be successful enough, accumulate enough, and everything is vulnerable. So the culture is really telling us that we live in a dangerous place and during dangerous times. I always wonder what humanity would be like if we were more respectful of humanity's need for safety.

Serge Prengel: So what you're saying is that it is not so much an intellectual shift or an emotional shift about simply paying attention to safety, but it's changing into a different system, voluntarily fostering the ability to shift into the social engagement system.

Dr. Porges: Yes, but let's qualify your statement to acknowledge that this shift to and from the social engagement system may not be voluntary. It might be more reflexive and driven by the cues in the social interaction as well as in the physical environment.

If we are smart—and this is where science can be helpful—we can start learning what features in the environment functionally trigger our nervous system into fight/flight or allow us to move into a state of safety and recruit the social engagement system, and what features in the environment trigger a behavioral shutdown, immobilization with fear, and states of dissociation. Often background noises can trigger a physiological state of mobilization and disrupt social interactions and feelings of safety. I have noticed that several clinical offices are in buildings with disruptive sounds, including the low-frequency sounds of ventilation systems and the mechanicals of large buildings. These sounds can interfere with the client's ability to progress.

Serge Prengel: I mean, if you are in New York City.

Dr. Porges: Yes. You might have heard on this phone call sounds of a train; it was the elevated train or "L," as we call it in Chicago. The train was producing physical cues to our nervous system to be vigilant and to anticipate potential danger. Often we are not aware of how our nervous system is bombarded with cues to be defensive. A "neurobiologically informed" design of an environment for humans would make sure that we lived, worked, and played in contexts without these features. Removing these forms of stimulation reduce the demands on our nervous system to be hypervigilant for predator or for danger. With these forms of stimulation removed, we could more easily functionally relax, engage, and get all the benefits of a social interaction.

But the real question is, how do we behave and feel when we no longer have the cues that trigger hypervigilance? Safe environments are important for everything we do and especially for therapies. I started to think about mindfulness meditation and realized that even mindfulness meditation exercises need to be conducted in a safe environment. It becomes obvious when you ask questions about how breathing and attention are influenced by background sounds and how easily we can become distracted and hypervigilant. I also realized that recruiting the defensive systems associated with sympathetic nervous system activation was incompatible with mindfulness. Perhaps a simple way of understanding this point is to realize that mindfulness requires a state that is nonjudgmental. However, this would be incompatible with states of defense in which evaluation is critical for survival. We can map this onto the Polyvagal Theory. Evaluation is really the same thing as saying we are in a dangerous environment and we need to sacrifice social engagement behaviors to ensure that we are hypervigilant and poised for fight and flight behaviors.

When we encourage our children to study and to attend to computer monitors, we are basically recruiting a hypervigilant state that is slightly modified to provide a state of focused sustained attention. However, this is not a state that supports health, growth, and restoration, nor does it support the social engagement behaviors necessary for successful social interactions.

The flip side is to understand the prerequisite features that enable us to feel safe and to turn off defensiveness. This leads to the exciting future of clinical treatments. If we were more understanding of the features in the environment that are capable of turning off the defensive systems, then clinical practices and clinical treatments would be more efficient. If the environment we lived in had the triggers for defense removed and replaced with features that trigger safety, then life would be healthier and of a higher quality. Several features could relatively easily be improved in our work and living environments. These would include reducing low-frequency noises in the environment, reducing the unpredictability of the environment, and simply being in proximity to people with whom you feel safe.

Serge Prengel: So, in a way, evolving toward treating underlying causes as opposed to treating symptoms.

Dr. Porges: We have different neural circuits that evolved with different but still profoundly important adaptive functions. As these neurophysiological systems evolved, they provided neural platforms for emergent behaviors, with each behavior having an adaptive function. I do not like to conceptualize behaviors as good or bad but view each behavior as sitting on a neural platform that represents the organism's attempt to adaptively survive. However, although this model enables behaviors to be conceptualized as adaptive, some behaviors interfere with appropriate social behavior and social interactions. Thus, a goal of therapy would be to enable clients to regulate their visceral state and to engage and to enjoy interactions with others. These social behaviors require that newest neural circuit regulating the autonomic nervous system. The neural circuit is unique to mammals and is available only when we feel safe. It is this system that not only facilitates social interaction and enables social interaction to foster growth, health, and restoration, but also has the capacity to down-regulate our reactions and the neural circuits that evolved for defense.

Serge Prengel: So we no longer are talking in terms of traditional pathologies but are talking about things that, in a way, are good reactions to possibly bad perceptions or basically regulating the way we function.

Dr. Porges: Yes, but I tend not to use the word "perception," because that involves a degree of awareness and cognition. We respond to features in our environment with physiological shifts that are outside the realm of awareness. I call this process neuroception to emphasize that the process is on a neural basis. Our body functions very much like a polygraph. Our body is continuously responding to people and places. We need to learn more about how to read our body's responses. We have to know that when we feel uncomfortable, there's a reason our body is feeling uncomfortable, and we need to adapt and adjust to that.

Serge Prengel: Except—to play devil's advocate—I would argue with the sense of reading the information, because that, again, would be a cognitive process.

Dr. Porges: You are absolutely right. It's a conundrum, isn't it?

Serge Prengel: It's hard to talk about processes without having these images.

Dr. Porges: I think we can wiggle out of this problem by merely saying that we need to respect our body's reactions rather than continually trying to develop the skill set that rejects whatever our body is telling us. When we respect our body's reactions, we can use our awareness and our voluntary behavior to navigate into places where we would feel more comfortable. With this new understanding, we can create a partnership between our own bodily feelings and our stewardship of the body via cognitive functions.

Serge Prengel: As I hear you, that language evokes a visual of gentle as opposed to jagged movement.

Dr. Porges: When we were young, we could deal with noisy places like bars or crowded rooms. But as we mature, we have difficulties understanding voices and relating to people when we are in noisy and crowded places. In a sense, our nervous system functionally starts to fail us. We want to escape from these uncomfortable environments. Many people have similar experiences. However, those who have these experiences do not, in a sense, respect the uncomfortable bodily reactions until it's too late and they can no longer control their behavior.

Serge Prengel: So, in a way, a lot of our pathologies come from too great an ability to override those signals.

Dr. Porges: We get the signals, but we do not respect them. I think this strategy of denying our bodily reactions has much to with our culture. This point is related to my introductory comment on Descartes, which emphasized a subjugation of bodily feelings to cognitive functions. Our culture's interdependence on religious views has contributed to dispelling the importance of bodily feelings. Specifically, bodily feelings were conceptualized as being associated with animals, while cognitions were an attribution more closely linked to spirit.

Serge Prengel: So we get to that sense of conceiving who we are from a bottom-up perspective.

Dr. Porges: But it is really both a bottom-up and a top-down model. We want to maintain the bidirectionality of mind–body or brain–viscera connection, because our brain is regulating our viscera and the viscera are continuously providing information to the brain. Simple movements, such as shifts in posture, result in changes in the signals our brain receives. When we lean forward or backward, we change our blood pressure and send different information to the baroreceptors, receptors that monitor blood pressure and communicate with areas in the brain.

When we lean back, we tend to become more relaxed and less aware of our environment. If we move to an upright position, we trigger a change in blood pressure that makes us feel more alert and focused. Thus, these simple behavioral manipulations, which trigger blood pressure receptors, can functionally change our interactions with the world.

In our basement, we have a chair that reclines and takes all the pressure off the lumbar region. When I am in this chair, I don't want to get out of it. I feel totally relaxed and don't want to do any work or think. I just want to be there. But when I go up to my office and sit in my desk, I am in the upright posture. My motivation and outlook change. When sitting at my desk, I start to see work as interesting and enjoyable. It is as if the shift in posture results in two different interactions with the environment. It is as if the psychological experiences reflect two different personalities: one lethargic and the other engaged and enthusiastic. So something as simple as a slight shift in posture can, by triggering neurophysiological circuits, change how we react to the world, how we organize thoughts, and how we motivate ourselves.

Serge Prengel: And what's interesting here is that this is caused by a shift in posture, which may also cause a shift in the dyad between, say, me and the environment.

Dr. Porges: Actually, you are onto something important. Another way of viewing it is our shifting from being focused on regulating the smooth muscles of our viscera in the relaxed state to recruiting striated muscles of our trunk and limbs in a more alert state. This occurs because sitting upright requires an increase in muscle tone. To accomplish this task, we need to recruit different neural circuits than when we are reclining and the tone of our striated muscles is relaxed. In the reclined position, we become literally a smooth muscle organism, which has an agenda to conserve resources. But, when we are in the upright posture, our skeletal muscles are required to maintain muscle tone, and we can now become an interactive, engaging organism.

Serge Prengel: So, in a philosophical way, you think of the individual, the self, as a process, and under certain circumstances, the process becomes oriented toward maintaining smooth muscles and fostering a state of relaxation.

Dr. Porges: When you experience a relaxed, immobilized state, specific physiological processes may occur that would support health, growth, and restoration. This is a very important and useful state, although it does not support social interactions or expansive thinking.

Serge Prengel: So, in a way, we're just talking about the way in which we can employ different neural circuits that enable us to react to and adapt to the dynamic changes in the environment.

Dr. Porges: If we conceptualize different neural platforms that support different domains of behavior, we can start to interpret the behaviors and the limitations of these behaviors within different neural platforms. When I am reclining, it's not that my lack of social behavior is maladaptive, but it would be viewed as maladaptive if I had a group of friends over for the evening. So the context is really defining what is appropriately adaptive. But the behaviors are emergent properties of the neural platform, and the adaptive characteristics are dependent on the appropriateness of these behaviors within a specific context. Conceptualizing behavior in these terms may change our understanding of behavioral pathologies. We might end up interpreting a behavioral pathology as a behavior that might have been adaptive in one setting and is now being elicited in a setting where it is maladaptive. For example, trauma survivors, who may be dissociating or shutting down, may be expressing a reaction that would be adaptive during the traumatic event but is maladaptive in a social setting.

Serge Prengel: So, in a sense, you are changing the definition of pathology to whether or not a behavior is adaptive in the current context.

Dr. Porges: I totally agree with that, and I think once we do that, behavior is neither good nor bad. It is just behavior that doesn't fit the context. This will enable us to take away some of the moral labels that have affected people who have difficulties regulating state to access the neural platforms that would support more appropriate behaviors.

Serge Prengel: And it's very, very important, very powerful, to take away that stigma, take away the moral context and judgment evaluation in a way that puts us in a mode of danger.

Dr. Porges: You are really getting at the core of the theory and how the theory can be distilled into very simple constructs related to our quest for safety. If we are not safe, we are chronically in a state of evaluation and defensiveness. However, if we can engage the circuits that support social engagement, we can regulate the neural platform that enables social engagement behaviors to spontaneously emerge. From a Polyvagal perspective, this would be the objective of therapy.

Serge Prengel: So this is a view that is about just understanding that these are processes that have a certain, apparent flow, and redirecting, learning, and in a way working with that potential that we have to learn and adapt.

Dr. Porges: You brought up another important point. That is, even though we have those three circuits to regulate state, we can modify the two defensive circuits through the use of this newer mammalian, social engagement system that is available when we are safe. Thus, once we can easily engage the social engagement system, we are free to mobilize without being in fight or flight. Rather than fight or flee, we can move and play. Although fight/flight and play behaviors both require mobilization, play turns off defensiveness by maintaining face-to-face social referencing.

Play uses the social engagement system to signal that the intentionality of the movements is not dangerous or hurtful. You can see this when dogs play. They chase each other and may mildly bite the other, and then they make face-to-face contact and reverse roles. If we watch people when they play sports, if they hit someone while playing, they will diffuse the aggressive reaction by making good eye contact and social communication. However, if they hit someone accidentally and walk away without defusing the valence of the action, a fight might occur. Similarly, the immobilization circuit may also be co-opted by the social engagement circuit during loving behavior that may initially start with face-to-face interactions that are followed by an immobilized state without fear. Over time, we become able to immobilize in the arms of another. I keep emphasizing the important role of immobilization without fear, because for mammals, immobilization is potentially lethal. So mammals are always moving unless they can feel safe with another.

Serge Prengel: Are we talking about the good immobilization?

Dr. Porges: Yes. The "good" immobilization response, immobilization without fear, requires the co-opting of the neural pathways involved in "immobilization with fear" with features of the social engagment system and neuropeptides, such as oxytocin. Functionally, oxytocin has receptors in the brainstem dorsal nucleus of the vagus that regulates the phylogenetically older unmyelinated vagus. This system of immobilization without fear enables women to give birth without fainting or dying. The same "good" immobilization system enables people to cuddle and hug without problems and enables women to breastfeed without having to move. Phylogenetically older structures, which initially evolved for defense, have been co-opted for play, reproduction and intimacy.

Serge Prengel: So what we do in therapy is in a way part of continuing that ability to adapt to structures.

Dr. Porges: I agree that the goal of therapy is to enable clients to experience greater flexibility in the world by having access to neural circuits that can efficiently dampen defense in appropriate settings and to utilize the phylogenetically older circuits for very positive outcomes.

Serge Prengel: Thanks, Stephen.

REFERENCES

Austin, M. A., Riniolo, T. C., & Porges, S. W. (2007). Borderline personality disorder and emotion regulation: Insights from the Polyvagal Theory. *Brain and cognition*, *65*(1), 69-76.

Borg, E., & Counter, S. A. (1989). The middle-ear muscles. *Sci Am*, *261*(2), 74-80.

Darwin, C. (1872). *The Expression of Emotions in Man and Animals*. London: John Murray.

Descartes, R. (1637). *Discourse on method and meditations* (L. J. Lafleur, trans.). New York, NY: Liberal Arts Press. Original work published

Hall, C. S. (1934). Emotional behavior in the rat: I. Defecation and urination as measures of individual differences in emotionality. *Journal of Comparative psychology*, *18*(3), 385.

Hering, H. E. (1910). A functional test of heart vagi in man. *Menschen Munchen Medizinische Wochenschrift*, *57*, 1931–1933.

Hughlings Jackson, J. (1884). On the evolution and dissolution of the nervous system. Croonian lectures 3, 4, and 5 to the Royal Society of London. Lancet, 1, 555-739.

Lewis, G. F., Furman, S. A., McCool, M. F., & Porges, S. W. (2012). Statistical strategies to quantify respiratory sinus arrhythmia: are commonly used metrics equivalent?. *Biological psychology, 89*(2), 349-364.

Ogden, P., Minton, K., & Pain, C. (2006). Trauma and the body: A Sensorimotor approach to psychotherapy. New York, NY: W. W. Norton & Co., Inc.

Porges, S. W. (1972). Heart rate variability and deceleration as indexes of reaction time. *Journal of Experimental Psychology, 92*(1), 103-110.

Porges, S. W. (1973). Heart rate variability: An autonomic correlate of reaction time performance. *Bulletin of the Psychonomic Society, 1*(4), 270-272.

Porges, S. W. (1985). *U.S. Patent No. 4,510,944*. Washington, DC: U.S. Patent and Trademark Office.

Porges, S. W. (1992). Vagal tone: a physiologic marker of stress vulnerability. *Pediatrics, 90*(3), 498-504.

Porges, S. W. (2003). The infant's sixth sense: Awareness and regulation of of bodily processes. Zero to Three: Bulletin of the National Center for Clinical Infant Programs 14:12–16.

Porges, S. W. (1995). Orienting in a defensive world: Mammalian modifications of our evolutionary heritage: A polyvagal theory. *Psychophysiology, 32*(4), 301–318.

Porges, S. W. (1998). Love: An emergent property of the mammalian autonomic nervous system. *Psychoneuroendocrinology, 23*(8), 837–861.

Porges, S. W. (2003). Social engagement and attachment. *Annals of the New York Academy of Sciences, 1008*(1), 31–47.

Porges, S. W. (2004). Neuroception: A Subconscious System for Detecting Threats and Safety. *Zero to Three (J), 24*(5), 19-24.

Porges, S. W. (2007). The polyvagal perspective. *Biological Psychology, 74*(2), 116–143.

Porges, S. W. (2011). The polyvagal theory: Neurophysiological foundations of emotions, attachment, communication, and self-regulation. Norton series on interpersonal neurobiology. New York, NY: W. W. Norton & Co., Inc.

Porges, S. W., & Lewis, G. F. (2010). .The polyvagal hypothesis: common mechanisms mediating autonomic regulation, vocalizations and listening. *Handbook of Behavioral Neuroscience, 19*, 255-264.

Porges, S. W., & Lewis, G. F. (2011). *U.S. Patent Application No. 13/992,450.*

Porges, S. W., Macellaio, M., Stanfill, S. D., McCue, K., Lewis, G. F., Harden, E. R., Handelman, M., Denver, J., Bazhenova, O.V., & Heilman, K. J. (2013). Respiratory sinus arrhythmia and auditory processing in autism: Modifiable deficits of an integrated social engagement system?. *International Journal of Psychophysiology, 88*(3), 261-270.

Porges, S. W., Bazhenova, O. V., Bal, E., Carlson, N., Sorokin, Y., Heilman, K. J., Cook, E. H. & Lewis, G. F. (2014). Reducing auditory hypersensitivities in autistic spectrum disorder: preliminary findings evaluating the listening project protocol. *Frontiers in Pediatrics.* doi:10.3389/fped.2014.00080

Porges, S. W. & Raskin, D. C. (1969). Respiratory and heart rate components of attention. *Journal of Experimental Psychology.* 81:497–501

Siegel;. D. J. (1999). The developing mind. New York: Guilford.

Stewart, A. M., Lewis, G. F., Heilman, K. J., Davila, M. I., Coleman, D. D., Aylward, S. A., & Porges, S. W. (2013). The covariation of acoustic features of infant cries and autonomic state. *Physiology & behavior, 120*, 203-210.

Stewart, A. M., Lewis, G. F., Yee, J. R., Kenkel, W. M., Davila,

M. I., Carter, C. S., & Porges, S. W. (2015). Acoustic features of prairie vole (Microtus ochrogaster) ultrasonic vocalizations covary with heart rate. *Physiology & behavior, 138*, 94-100.

Stern, J. A. (1964). Toward a definition of psychophysiology. *Psychophysiology, 1*(1), 90–91.

Woodworth, R. S. (1929). *Psychology*. New York, NY: Holt.

Wiener, N. (1954). The human use of human beings: Cybernetics and society (No. 320) Da Capo Press.

ADDITIONAL POLYVAGAL THEORY REFERENCES

Bal, E., Harden, E., Lamb, D., Van Hecke, A. V., Denver, J. W., & Porges, S. W. (2010). Emotion recognition in children with autism spectrum disorders: Relations to eye gaze and autonomic state. *Journal of autism and developmental disorders, 40*(3), 358-370.

Carter, C. S., & Porges, S. W. (2013). The biochemistry of love: an oxytocin hypothesis. *EMBO reports, 14*(1), 12-16.

Dale, L. P., Carroll, L. E., Galen, G., Hayes, J. A., Webb, K. W., & Porges, S. W. (2009). Abuse history is related to autonomic regulation to mild exercise and psychological well-being. *Applied psychophysiology and biofeedback, 34*(4), 299-308.

Flores, P. J., & Porges, S. W. (2017). Group Psychotherapy as a Neural Exercise: Bridging Polyvagal Theory and Attachment Theory. *International Journal of Group Psychotherapy, 67*(2), 202–222.

Geller, S. M., & Porges, S. W. (2014). Therapeutic presence: Neurophysiological mechanisms mediating feeling safe in therapeutic relationships. *Journal of Psychotherapy Integration, 24*(3), 178.

Grippo, A. J., Lamb, D. G., Carter, C. S., & Porges, S. W. (2007). Cardiac regulation in the socially monogamous prairie vole. *Physiology & behavior, 90*(2), 386-393.

Grippo, A. J., Lamb, D. G., Carter, C. S., & Porges, S. W. (2007). Social isolation disrupts autonomic regulation of the heart and influences negative affective behaviors. *Biological psychiatry, 62*(10), 1162-1170.

Heilman, K. J., Bal, E., Bazhenova, O. V., & Porges, S. W. (2007). Respiratory sinus arrhythmia and tympanic membrane compliance predict spontaneous eye gaze behaviors in young children: A pilot study. *Developmental Psychobiology, 49*(5), 531-542.

Heilman, K. J., Connolly, S. D., Padilla, W. O., Wrzosek, M. I., Graczyk, P. A., & Porges, S. W. (2012). Sluggish vagal brake reactivity to physical exercise challenge in children with selective mutism. *Development and Psychopathology, 24*(01), 241-250.

Heilman, K. J., Harden, E. R., Weber, K. M., Cohen, M., & Porges, S. W. (2013). Atypical autonomic regulation, auditory processing, and affect recognition in women with HIV. *Biological psychology, 94*(1), 143-151.

Jones, R. M., Buhr, A. P., Conture, E. G., Tumanova, V., Walden, T. A., & Porges, S. W. (2014). Autonomic nervous system activity of preschool-age children who stutter. *Journal of fluency disorders, 41*, 12-31.

Kenkel, W. M., Paredes, J., Lewis, G. F., Yee, J. R., Pournajafi-Nazarloo, H., Grippo, A. J., Porges, S.W., & Carter, C. S. (2013). Autonomic substrates of the response to pups in male prairie voles. *PloS one, 8*(8), e69965.

Patriquin, M. A., Scarpa, A., Friedman, B. H., & Porges, S. W. (2013). Respiratory sinus arrhythmia: A marker for positive social functioning and receptive language skills in children with autism spectrum disorders. *Developmental Psychobiology, 55*(2), 101-112.

Porges, S. W. (1997). Emotion: an evolutionary by-product of the neural regulation of the autonomic nervous system. *Annals of the New York Academy of Sciences, 807*(1), 62-77.

Porges, S. W. (2001). The polyvagal theory: phylogenetic substrates of a social nervous system. *International Journal of Psychophysiology, 42*(2), 123-146.

Porges, S. W. (2003). The polyvagal theory: Phylogenetic contributions to social behavior. *Physiology & Behavior, 79*(3), 503-513.

Porges, S. W. (2005). The vagus: A mediator of behavioral and visceral features associated with autism. In ML Bauman and TL Kemper, eds. *The Neurobiology of Autism.* Baltimore: Johns Hopkins University Press, 65-78.

Porges, S. W. (2005). The role of social engagement in attachment and bonding: A phylogenetic perspective. In CS Carter, L Ahnert, K Grossmann K, SB Hrdy, ME Lamb, SW Porges, N Sachser, eds. *Attachment and Bonding: A New Synthesis (92)* Cambridge, MA: MIT Press, pp. 33-54.

Porges, S. W. (2009). The polyvagal theory: new insights into adaptive reactions of the autonomic nervous system. *Cleveland Clinic journal of medicine, 76*(Suppl 2), S86.

Porges, S. W. (2015). Making the world safe for our children: Down-regulating defence and up-regulating social engagement to 'optimise' the human experience. *Children Australia, 40*(02), 114-123.

Porges, S. W., & Furman, S. A. (2011). The early development of the autonomic nervous system provides a neural platform for social behaviour: A polyvagal perspective. *Infant and child development, 20*(1), 106-118.

Porges, S. W., Doussard-Roosevelt, J. A., Portales, A. L., & Greenspan, S. I. (1996). Infant regulation of the vagal "brake" predicts child behavior problems: A psychobiological model of social behavior. *Developmental psychobiology, 29*(8), 697-712.

Reed, S. F., Ohel, G., David, R., & Porges, S. W. (1999). A neural explanation of fetal heart rate patterns: A test of the Polyvagal Theory. *Developmental Psychobiology*. 35:108–118.

Williamson, J. B., Porges, E. C., Lamb, D. G., & Porges, S. W. (2015). Maladaptive autonomic regulation in PTSD accelerates physiological aging. *Frontiers in psychology, 5*, 1571.

Williamson, J. B., Heilman, K. M., Porges, E., Lamb, D., & Porges, S. W. (2013). A possible mechanism for PTSD symptoms in patients with traumatic brain injury: central autonomic network disruption. *Frontiers in neuroengineering, 6*, 13.

Williamson, J. B., Lewis, G., Grippo, A. J., Lamb, D., Harden, E., Handleman, M., Lebow, J., Carter, C. S., & Porges, S. W. (2010). Autonomic predictors of recovery following surgery: a comparative study. *Autonomic Neuroscience, 156*(1), 60-6

Yee, J. R., Kenkel, W. M., Frijling, J. L., Dodhia, S., Onishi, K. G., Tovar, S, Saber. M. J., Lewis, G.F., Liu, W., Porges, S.W., & Carter, C. S. (2016). Oxytocin promotes functional coupling between paraventricular nucleus and both sympathetic and parasympathetic cardioregulatory nuclei. *Hormones and behavior, 80*, 82-91.

CREDITS

Chapter 2: This interview was revised by Stephen W. Porges for this book edition. The original interview occurred in April 2011. Copyright © by Stephen W. Porges & NICABM (National Institute for the Clinical Application of Behavioral Medicine, Storrs, CT). Website: www.nicabm.com

Chapter 3: This interview was revised by Stephen W. Porges for this book edition. The original interview occurred in April 2012. Copyright © by Stephen W. Porges & NICABM (National Institute for the Clinical Application of Behavioral Medicine, Storrs, CT). Website: www.nicabm.com

Chapter 4: This interview was revised by Stephen W. Porges for this book edition. The original interview occurred in February and March 2013. Copyright © by Stephen W. Porges & NICABM (National Institute for the Clinical Application of Behavioral Medicine, Storrs, CT). Website: www.nicabm.com

Chapter 5: This interview was revised by Stephen W. Porges for this book edition. The original interview occurred in March 2014. Copyright © by Stephen W. Porges & NICABM (National Institute for the Clinical Application of Behavioral Medicine, Storrs, CT). Website: www.nicabm.com

Chapter 6: This interview was revised by Stephen W. Porges for this book edition. The original was created in the winter

Also available from

THE NORTON SERIES ON INTERPERSONAL NEUROBIOLOGY

The Birth of Intersubjectivity: Psychodynamics, Neurobiology, and the Self

Massimo Ammaniti, Vittorio Gallese

Neurobiology for Clinical Social Work: Theory and Practice (Second Edition)

Jeffrey S. Applegate, Janet R. Shapiro

Mind–Brain–Gene

John B. Arden

The Heart of Trauma: Healing the Embodied Brain in the Context of Relationships

Bonnie Badenoch

Being a Brain-Wise Therapist: A Practical Guide to Interpersonal Neurobiology

Bonnie Badenoch

The Brain-Savvy Therapist's Workbook

Bonnie Badenoch

The Neurobiology of Attachment-Focused Therapy

Jonathan Baylin, Daniel A. Hughes

Coping with Trauma-Related Dissociation: Skills Training for Patients and Therapists

Suzette Boon, Kathy Steele, and Onno van der Hart

Neurobiologically Informed Trauma Therapy with Children and Adolescents: Understanding Mechanisms of Change

Linda Chapman

Intensive Psychotherapy for Persistent Dissociative Processes: The Fear of Feeling Real

RICHARD A. CHEFETZ

Timeless: Nature's Formula for Health and Longevity

LOUIS COZOLINO

The Neuroscience of Human Relationships: Attachment and the Developing Social Brain (Second Edition)

LOUIS COZOLINO

The Neuroscience of Psychotherapy: Healing the Social Brain (Second Edition)

LOUIS COZOLINO

Why Therapy Works: Using Our Minds to Change Our Brains

LOUIS COZOLINO

From Axons to Identity: Neurological Explorations of the Nature of the Self

TODD E. FEINBERG

Loving with the Brain in Mind: Neurobiology and Couple Therapy

MONA DEKOVEN FISHBANE

Body Sense: The Science and Practice of Embodied Self-Awareness

ALAN FOGEL

The Healing Power of Emotion: Affective Neuroscience, Development & Clinical Practice

DIANA FOSHA, DANIEL J. SIEGEL, MARION SOLOMON

Healing the Traumatized Self: Consciousness, Neuroscience, Treatment

PAUL FREWEN, RUTH LANIUS

The Neuropsychology of the Unconscious: Integrating Brain and Mind in Psychotherapy

Efrat Ginot

10 Principles for Doing Effective Couples Therapy

Julie Schwartz Gottman and John M. Gottman

The Impact of Attachment

Susan Hart

Art Therapy and the Neuroscience of Relationships, Creativity, and Resiliency: Skills and Practices

Noah Hass-Cohen and Joanna Clyde Findlay

Affect Regulation Theory: A Clinical Model

Daniel Hill

Brain-Based Parenting: The Neuroscience of Caregiving for Healthy Attachment

Daniel A. Hughes, Jonathan Baylin

Sex Addiction as Affect Dysregulation: A Neurobiologically Informed Holistic Treatment

Alexandra Katehakis

The Interpersonal Neurobiology of Play: Brain-Building Interventions for Emotional Well-Being

Theresa A. Kestly

Self-Agency in Psychotherapy: Attachment, Autonomy, and Intimacy

Jean Knox

Infant/Child Mental Health, Early Intervention, and Relationship-Based Therapies: A Neurorelational Framework for Interdisciplinary Practice

Connie Lillas, Janiece Turnbull

Play and Creativity in Psychotherapy

Terry Marks-Tarlow, Marion Solomon, Daniel J. Siegel

Clinical Intuition in Psychotherapy: The Neurobiology of Embodied Response

Terry Marks-Tarlow

Awakening Clinical Intuition: An Experiential Workbook for Psychotherapists

Terry Marks-Tarlow

A Dissociation Model of Borderline Personality Disorder

Russell Meares

Borderline Personality Disorder and the Conversational Model: A Clinician's Manual

Russell Meares

Neurobiology Essentials for Clinicians: What Every Therapist Needs to Know

Arlene Montgomery

Borderline Bodies: Affect Regulation Therapy for Personality Disorders

Clara Mucci

Neurobiology and the Development of Human Morality: Evolution, Culture, and Wisdom

Darcia Narvaez

Brain Model & Puzzle: Anatomy & Functional Areas of the Brain

Norton Professional Books

Sensorimotor Psychotherapy: Interventions for Trauma and Attachment

Pat Ogden, Janina Fisher

Trauma and the Body: A Sensorimotor Approach to Psychotherapy

PAT OGDEN, KEKUNI MINTON, CLARE PAIN

The Archaeology of Mind: Neuroevolutionary Origins of Human Emotions

JAAK PANKSEPP, LUCY BIVEN

The Polyvagal Theory: Neurophysiological Foundations of Emotions, Attachment, Communication, and Self-regulation

STEPHEN W. PORGES

The Pocket Guide to Polyvagal Theory: The Transformative Power of Feeling Safe

STEPHEN W. PORGES

Foundational Concepts in Neuroscience: A Brain-Mind Odyssey

DAVID E. PRESTI

Right Brain Psychotherapy

ALLAN N. SCHORE

The Development of the Unconscious Mind

ALLAN N. SCHORE

Affect Dysregulation and Disorders of the Self

ALLAN N. SCHORE

Affect Regulation and the Repair of the Self

ALLAN N. SCHORE

The Science of the Art of Psychotherapy

ALLAN N. SCHORE

Mind: A Journey to the Heart of Being Human

DANIEL J. SIEGEL

The Mindful Brain: Reflection and Attunement in the Cultivation of Well-Being

DANIEL J. SIEGEL

The Mindful Therapist: A Clinician's Guide to Mindsight and Neural Integration

DANIEL J. SIEGEL

Pocket Guide to Interpersonal Neurobiology: An Integrative Handbook of the Mind

DANIEL J. SIEGEL

Healing Moments in Psychotherapy

DANIEL J. SIEGEL, MARION SOLOMON

Healing Trauma: Attachment, Mind, Body and Brain

DANIEL J. SIEGEL, MARION SOLOMON

Love and War in Intimate Relationships: Connection, Disconnection, and Mutual Regulation in Couple Therapy

MARION SOLOMON, STAN TATKIN

How People Change: Relationships and Neuroplasticity in Psychotherapy

MARION SOLOMON AND DANIEL J. SIEGEL

The Present Moment in Psychotherapy and Everyday Life

DANIEL N. STERN

The Neurobehavioral and Social-Emotional Development of Infants and Children

ED TRONICK

The Haunted Self: Structural Dissociation and the Treatment of Chronic Traumatization

ONNO VAN DER HART, ELLERT R. S. NIJENHUIS, KATHY STEELE

Prenatal Development and Parents' Lived Experiences: How Early Events Shape Our Psychophysiology and Relationships

ANN DIAMOND WEINSTEIN

Changing Minds in Therapy: Emotion, Attachment, Trauma, and Neurobiology

MARGARET WILKINSON

For all the latest books in the series, book details (including sample chapters), and to order online, please visit the Series webpage at wwnorton.com/Psych/IPNB Series

ABOUT THE AUTHOR

Stephen W. Porges, Ph.D., is Distinguished University Scientist at Indiana University where he is the founding director of the Traumatic Stress Research Consortium. He is Professor of Psychiatry at the University of North Carolina, and Professor Emeritus at both the University of Illinois at Chicago and the University of Maryland. He served as president of the Society for Psychophysiological Research and the Federation of Associations in Behavioral & Brain Sciences and is a former recipient of a National Institute of Mental Health Research Scientist Development Award. He is the originator of the Polyvagal Theory and has published more than 300 peer-reviewed scientific papers across several disciplines.